W0007651

NDS OF THE

EARLY CHRISTIAN

STORY

Troas

ASIA

Ephesus

Miletus

Rhodes

Attalia

Myra

Iconium

Lystra

CAPPADOCIA

Tarsus

Antioch

CYPRUS

Paphos

Salamis

SYRIA

Damascus

SEA

Tyre

Galilee

Caesarea

Jerusalem

Judaea

ARABIA

Alexandria

EGYPT

THE BIBLE STORY
AND ITS BACKGROUND

Book Seven
THE CHURCH OF JESUS BEGINS

THE BIBLE STORY AND ITS BACKGROUND   Book Seven

The Church of Jesus Begins

Revised Edition

NORMAN BULL, M.A., Ph.D.
Illustrated by Grace Golden, A.R.C.A.

HULTON EDUCATIONAL

Foreword to the Second Edition

The first four books in this series trace the story of the Jewish people and their faith, as told in the Old Testament. The remainder of the series is devoted to the New Testament—the life and teachings of Jesus Christ, the work of Paul the Apostle and the early years of the Christian church. In this way the entire span of Bible times is covered. The period extends from about 2000 B.C.E. (2000 B.C.) to C.E. 66 (A.D. 66) and the main events and outstanding figures are described.

Within this chronological framework there is an illuminating commentary on the contemporary scene. The geographical setting, the political background, the successive kingdoms and rulers are described, as are the customs, occupations and day-to-day life of rich and poor. The many illustrations portray these details with great vividness. There are Bible references to be looked up, and frequent assignments related to the text.

The author's aim is to show the Bible story in its true historical setting. In a style which is direct and simple he draws on his considerable knowledge to give added meaning and absorbing interest to this greatest of all books.

First published in Great Britain 1969
by Hulton Educational Publications Ltd
Raans Road, Amersham, Bucks HP6 6JJ

Reprinted 1973, 1978
Second edition 1984

Text © Norman Bull, 1969, 1984
Illustrations © Hulton Educational Publications Ltd, 1969

All rights reserved. No part of this publication may be reproduced, stored in a retrieval system, or transmitted in any form or by any means, electronic, mechanical, photocopying, recording or otherwise, without the prior written consent of Hulton Educational Publications Ltd

ISBN 0 7175 0983 4

Printed in Hong Kong by Wing King Tong Co. Ltd

CONTENTS

The World to which Christianity Came

Church

The word 'church' is used for the building in which Christians meet to worship God. CHURCH comes from the Greek word 'kuriakon' which means BELONGING TO THE LORD. A church is also a group of people, not only a building. The Christian Church, therefore, is the body of people, all over the world, who believe in Jesus as their Lord and therefore belong to him.

LORD is the translation of the Greek word 'Kurios'. It meant a supreme, all-powerful ruler. It was the word used for God in the Greek version of the Old Testament, the only Scriptures at that time. Thus to the Jews 'Lord' meant 'God'. Pagans used this word, too, for their gods. Romans used it as the title of the mighty Roman emperor, ruler of the world and lord of all. That is the reason why Christians used this word for Jesus. 'JESUS CHRIST IS LORD' (Philippians 2.11) summed up the faith of Christians.

The Christian Church began among some Jews. For long centuries the Jewish people had looked forward to a Golden Age for their nation. It would be set up by God. He would send a great ruler to his people, anointed by him just as a king was anointed. The 'Lord's Anointed' would be their heaven-sent leader. Now the happiest time that the Jews had ever known had been the reign of King David, a thousand years before the time of Jesus. Under him, their kingdom had been great and happy, and the twelve tribes of the Jews had been united. David's son, Solomon, had undone his father's work. When he died, ten of the tribes had revolted against his son and set up a separate kingdom in the north. But they had been conquered by the terrible Assyrians in the eighth century B.C.E. They had been taken off as captives, mixed with other peoples, and disappeared from history. That left only two tribes in the little kingdom of Judah in the south. They had been conquered by the Babylonians, and taken off into exile in Babylon in the sixth century B.C.E. When the Persians had conquered Babylon, they had been allowed to return to Judah. Now their tiny country was part of the great Persian Empire. Then, in the fourth century B.C.E., Alexander the Great had conquered a large portion of the ancient world. The Jews were now ruled by Greek kingdoms set up by Alexander's generals. Revolt against persecution had given them independence, for a time, under their own Maccabean rulers. But civil war had brought the Romans in 63 B.C.E.

ASSYRIAN

At first the Jews thought that, since David had been their greatest king, the great leader would come from the family of David. He would bring them peace and prosperity and power. But this never happened. They were conquered by one empire after another—Assyrian, Babylonian, Persian, Greek, Roman. Gradually their hope of an earthly king took on more and more aspects of a heavenly saviour as well. The Hebrew word for this deliverer was MESSIAH or ANOINTED ONE. The Greek word for this was CHRISTOS. This explains why those who believed in Jesus called him the CHRIST. From this comes the word CHRISTIANITY for the religion of faith in Jesus.

GREEK

BABYLONIAN

PERSIAN

ROMAN

THE HOLY LAND IN
ROMAN TIMES

km
0 10 20

MEDITERRANEAN SEA

PROVINCE OF SYRIA

Tyre

Caesarea Philippi

Tetrarchy
of Philip

GALILEE
Tetrarchy

SEA of GALILEE

Nazareth

CAESAREA

DECAPOLIS

SAMARIA

of Herod Antipas

Sebaste
(Samaria)

Gerasa

Philip

Procuracy of Pontius Pilate

R. JORDAN

PERAEA

Joppa

JERUSALEM

DEAD SEA

Herod

JUDAEA

Masada

Pilate

IDUMAEA

Thus the Christian Church began with a person, Jesus of Nazareth. He lived on earth from about 5 B.C.E. to C.E. 29. His followers were convinced that, after his death on the cross, they had experienced his living presence. They began to spread their faith in him and so the Christian Church was born. But Christianity came into the world at a certain time. We must know something about that world before we can understand how the Church grew. Many believe that the world had been prepared in a special way for the coming of Christianity.

The Romans

Christianity came into a world ruled by the Romans. Their mighty empire stretched from the Atlantic Ocean in the west, to the deserts of Arabia in the east, and from the north of Britain to the land of Egypt. It was divided up into thirty-six provinces, outside Italy, and its population was about fifty million people. Governors for these provinces were generally appointed for two years by the Roman Senate, the 'Parliament' of Rome. Some were appointed by the emperor himself, the commander-in-chief of the armies of

THE ROMAN EMPIRE
AT THE BIRTH OF JESUS

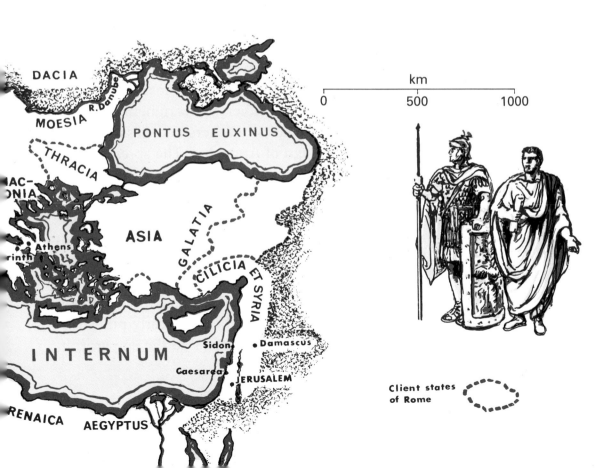

km
0   500   1000

Client states
of Rome

Rome. These were trouble spots where troops were always needed to keep order. Judaea had become part of the Roman empire in 63 B.C.E., and its people were always troublesome. The Romans had to ensure order in Judaea, for it flanked their eastern frontier, 1300 km long, beyond which were the fiery Parthians. They needed a strong ruler in Judaea and they found one in Herod the Great. But after his death, the emperor had to send Procurators to govern the Jews. Of these Pontius Pilate was the best known.

The Romans had built up their empire by long wars. First they had conquered Italy, then the Mediterranean power of Carthage, then the Greek kingdoms. These wars went on for a hundred years. Then followed another century of civil wars, when Roman leaders fought for power. It had ended when Augustus Caesar became sole ruler of the whole Roman world. His long reign, from 31 B.C.E to C.E. 15 brought peace and prosperity to the empire. Under the famous PAX ROMANA, Roman peace, the world enjoyed order and justice. Along the fine Roman roads, many of which remain to this day, passed Roman soldiers, government officials, regular posts, bankers and merchants, teachers and missionaries.

Jesus was born during the reign of Augustus. The spread of his Church was made possible by the peace, order and unity that Augustus had brought to the Roman world. Travel was safe for any law-abiding man throughout the empire. But to have ROMAN CITIZENSHIP was a high honour that placed anyone who possessed it under the direct protection of the emperor himself. Paul, the great Christian missionary, was a Roman citizen. Once he was arrested and the order was given for him to be flogged. The Roman officer was horrified when he found that he had nearly punished a Roman citizen. A citizen could always appeal to the emperor, if he were involved in any legal matter. Paul did this. Now his case was transferred directly to Rome. Now he could preach the Gospel of Jesus in the capital of the whole empire.

Emperor worship

Many people, especially in the east, began to pay divine honours to the great emperor Augustus. They began their year with his birthday, and they held religious festivals in his honour. It seems strange to us that a man should be worshipped as a god, however great he might be. But this custom was common in the ancient world. For many centuries the pharaohs of Egypt and the kings of Babylon had been worshipped as gods. Alexander the Great had thought of himself as divine, and the rulers of the Greek kingdoms that came after him had claimed divine honours.

THE TEMPLE OF AUGUSTUS, SAMARIA

(a reconstruction)

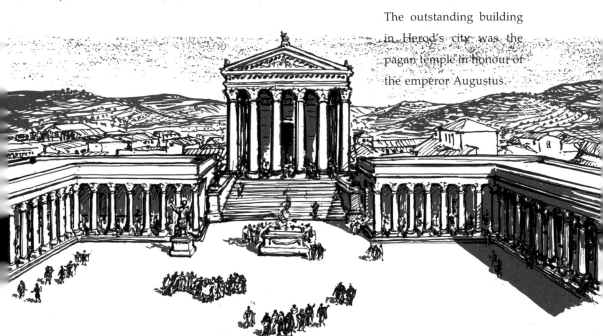

The outstanding building in Herod's city was the pagan temple in honour of the emperor Augustus.

Augustus Caesar, 31 B.C.E. to C.E. 14. Jesus was born during his reign.

Caligula, C.E. 37–41. A madman, he was finally assassinated.

Nero, C.E. 57–68, the first emperor to persecute Christians.

*Claudius Caesar
as a god.
(From a Roman statue)*

Tiberius Caesar, C.E. 14–37. Jesus was crucified during his reign.

Claudius, C.E. 41–57. He is mentioned in Acts 18.2.

Vespasian, C.E. 69–79, the emperor who joked on his deathbed about 'becoming a god'.

WORSHIP OF THE ROMAN EMPERORS

(Portraits from Roman coins)

Pagan religions regarded everything as divine—man, and nature, as well as gods. A man might well be a god in human form, especially if he were a great king or a mighty emperor. Paul and Barnabas, on one of their missionary journeys, were once taken as gods in human form. Usually rulers were paid divine honours after they had died. Some claimed them in their own lifetime. The rulers of Rome saw that reverence for the emperor would help to bind all the peoples of the empire together. They introduced this custom of worshipping rulers from the east to the west. Some emperors took it more seriously than others. Vespasian, a rough soldier, joked about it as he lay dying. 'I think I am becoming a god,' he said. But the emperor Domitian (C.E. 81–96) proclaimed himself DOMINUS AC DEUS NOSTER—OUR LORD AND GOD.

Worship of the emperor was very popular in the east of the empire. Special officials called ASIARCHS were appointed to organise special days in honour of the emperor and his divinity. There were all kinds of ceremonies and processions, festivals and games, held in his honour. Neither Jews nor Christians could ever join in them. Both believed in the one and only God, Creator and Lord of all. They could not worship either idols or men.

Roman religions

All the peoples of the Roman world, except for the Jews, believed in many gods—POLYTHEISM. The religion of the Jews was MONOTHEISM, belief in one God only. Because the Romans were polytheistic, they could accept all kinds of religions. The Roman world was full of all kinds of gods and goddesses.

In early times the Romans had household gods. There were the

A Lar

Altar

Dionysus

'lares', the spirits of family ancestors, and the 'penates' or guardians of the household. Some of these gods later became national gods. For example, Vesta, goddess of the hearth became goddess of the Roman state. They had gods of agriculture, too, who were believed to control seed and soil, water and weather, and the growing of crops. Sacrifices had to be made to them if men were to gather in good harvests. The life of men and beasts depended on the worship of the gods, too. Supreme amongst them was Jupiter, the sky god.

People who believed in many gods could easily identify one god with another. This happened between the gods of the Greeks and the Roman gods. Zeus became Jupiter, lord of all gods; Hermes, the winged messenger of the gods, became Mercury; Poseidon, Greek god of the seas, became the Roman god Neptune. As the Romans conquered new lands, and came to know new gods, they added these divinities to their Pantheon, home of all gods, in Rome. Gods from Asia Minor, from Egypt, from Syria, were included. Any new god was accepted, provided that he could be identified with a Roman god. Jews and Christians could not agree with this. For how could a man-made god or idol be united with the one living God?

Vesta

Roma,
Goddess of the
city of Rome

ROMAN GODS

Minerva, goddess of wisdom

Jupiter, lord of the gods

Juno, wife of Jupiter

Neptune, god of the sea

Ceres, goddess of agriculture

Mars, god of war

Such simple cults and superstitions did not satisfy thinking people. Nor could they seriously think of a half-crazy emperor as a god. Many fine Romans followed the Greek philosophy called STOICISM. Its founder was a Phoenician from Syria named Zeno. It took its name from the 'stoa' or 'porch' in Athens where he taught. Stoicism believed in a divine reason behind the universe. Men should live in tune with it, for they were free to choose how to live. A wicked man, said one Stoic, is like a dog tied to a cart—he has to follow evil. A good man, living by reason, would follow virtue and duty and self-discipline. He would never give way to passion. Virtue came from the will. Outward circumstances could never affect it. Suffering gave the best opportunity to practise virtue.

The Stoic way of life was a fine one, but it was hard and stern. From Stoicism came the four great virtues—Prudence, Justice, Temperance, Fortitude. These are called the *cardinal virtues* ('cardo'—'hinge'), for all other virtues hinged on them. Christians added to them the three virtues of Faith, Hope, Love. These are called the THEOLOGICAL VIRTUES ('theos'—'God'), for they come to us from God. But Christians had many things in common with Stoics. Both believed in the brotherhood of man, in virtue, in self-discipline, and in the emptiness of worldly things. Thus, Stoicism helped to prepare the way for Christianity. Many fine Roman officials lived by the Stoic philosophy. The writings of one Roman Stoic, named Seneca, became very popular among Christians.

Zeno

Seneca

Mystery religions

Stoicism could never be a popular way of living. It was too high and strict and difficult. Stoics were usually well-educated and serious-minded. Among the mass of the people there were popular religions which had come from the east. These were the MYSTERY RELIGIONS. They were strange cults which offered escape from a hard life and assurance of life after death. They came from old nature-religions. The Greek word 'mystes' meant originally 'one who shuts the eyes and mouth', keeping secrets. It came to mean an 'initiate', a new member, of these Mystery Religions. They were so secret that our knowledge of them is incomplete. Each was based on a 'myth', a divine story telling how a god or goddess ordered the world of nature. The myth was acted in the ceremony, telling dramatically what the god did. The initiate shared in the drama and so shared in the life of the god.

One famous mystery religion came from Eleusis, near Athens. Its meeting-place has been found by archaeologists. It was a hall that held 3000 people. In these Eleusian Mysteries, the myth was about Persephone, daughter of Zeus, the chief of the gods, and Demeter, the Greek goddess of agriculture. Pluto, god of the underworld, seized the maiden and carried her down to Hades. Her mother, Demeter, would not let the grain grow again until Persephone was returned to her. Pluto gave in, but first he gave Persephone a magic pomegranate seed, so that she would have to return to him for part of each year. That was winter. When Persephone came up each year the crops grew again, making spring and summer. Thus the myth explained the seasons of the year. It was acted in the Mysteries. The initiates, carefully prepared

23

beforehand, 'saw' the goddess and they were 'united' with her. Now they shared in her life and in her immortality. As she died and rose again, so would they. After this dramatic ceremony, the worshippers joined in a meal of fellowship together. Their religion brought them happiness in this life and hope for the life to come.

Another Mystery Religion was the cult of Mithras, which spread from Persia, through Asia Minor, to the west. Mithras was a hero-god, 'Sol Invictus', the Unconquerable Sun. Each day he conquered darkness and renewed his power. He was the enemy of darkness and of evil, a saviour who promised life after death with him in the heavens. In this cult the initiates went through a ceremony called the 'taurobolium', baptism in the blood of a bull. This hero religion became very popular among Roman soldiers, and it spread with the legions. A shrine of Mithras was found at Ostia, the port of Rome. Another has been discovered in the City of London.

MITHRAISM

A Mystery Religion which appealed especially to men, and spread through the Roman world with the legions.

Relief of Mithras slaying the Bull

Head of the god Mithras found in the London Temple

Inside a Mithraeum showing procession of worshippers in ceremonial costumes

Mithraeum in London

8 m

25

The Christian Church had some things in common with these Mystery Religions. It had a rite of initiation—baptism; a fellowship-meal—the Lord's Supper; and the promise of life after death, by sharing in the life of the Lord. But these were known in Judaism, from which Christianity had sprung. Christians did not copy these from the Mystery Religions.

The Mystery Religions, like the others, were found at the same time as Christianity. They were founded on folk tales. But Christianity was founded upon Jesus of Nazareth, who had lived on earth and been put to death by a Roman Procurator.

Hellenism

The Romans conquered the Greeks, just as they conquered every other people. But, in another way, the Romans were themselves conquered by the Greeks—by Greek culture and the Greek way of life.

The Romans were a practical people, good at physical things. They fought and conquered, organised and ruled, made laws and administered justice, built cities and roads. But much of their thought and culture, their religion and philosophy, were borrowed from the Greeks. HELLAS is the word for GREECE in the Greek language. From it comes the word HELLENISM, meaning the CULTURE OF GREECE. It had begun to spread all over the Mediterranean world, even before the Greek conquests of Alexander the Great in the fourth century B.C.E. By the time of Jesus, Greek culture was everywhere. Even in Judaea there was a league of Greek cities called the DECAPOLIS ('Ten Cities'), and we know that Jesus travelled near them. The ruins of one such place, Jerash, show how magnificent these Greek cities were.

GERASA, A HELLENISTIC CITY OF THE DECAPOLIS

The remains of theatre and forum

The city of Gerasa, or Jerash, lay about 64 km to the south-east of the Sea of Galilee, in modern Jordan. It has been called the 'Pompeii of the East', because its remains are so well preserved. They show what a magnificent city it must have been. It had been built by Greeks about the time of Alexander the Great, and rebuilt by the Romans mainly in the second and third centuries C.E. A triumphal arch led to the city walls, which were approximately 5 km round. Among the city's fine buildings were a temple of Dionysius, a temple of Artemis, a temple of Zeus, a theatre, an oval forum, and a Street of Columns, 520 in all; baths, a stadium, and a hippodrome with room for 15 000 spectators. The streets, carefully laid out, were lined with shops and adorned with fountains. In later times, Christian churches were made out of the stone-work of the pagan temples.

Paul, in one of his letters, divided men into two groups—Greeks and Barbarians (Romans 1.14). By 'Greeks' he meant, not those who were Greeks by birth, but those who shared the Greek way of life, no matter what their race. 'Barbarians' were all those who did not share Greek culture.

The spread of Greek culture went hand in hand with the spread of the Greek language. Latin was the official language of the Roman world. But KOINE ('common') or HELLENISTIC Greek, as it is known, was the universal language for nearly six centuries. About half a million Jews lived in the Holy Land, but over four millions were settled over the Mediterranean world. They all spoke Greek. In the third century B.C.E. the Jewish Scriptures, the Christian Old Testament, had been translated into Greek at Alexandria, where half the population were Jews. This SEPTUAGINT, as it is known, was used by all Jews outside the Holy Land, by the apostles, by Paul, and by the Christian Church. All the Christian Scriptures, the New Testament, were written in Greek, too. This fluent and graceful language could be both simple and subtle. It could be used for everyday speech as well as for teaching religion and philosophy. As a universal language it made possible the spread of the Christian Church. For, wherever they went, Christian missionaries could be understood.

Greek philosophy
The Greek mind was eager and enquiring. Greeks asked the deepest questions of all—about the nature of the universe, of man, and of God. This gave rise to PHILOSOPHY—LOVE OF WISDOM. Greek philosophy began about 500 B.C.E. and among its great thinkers

PHILOSOPHERS

Socrates

Plato

Aristotle

Marcus Aurelius

Zeno teaching in Athens

were Socrates, Plato, and Aristotle who had been tutor to Alexander the Great. Plato, in his philosophy, sought after 'The Good'. He taught that the highest ideas men can know are truth, beauty and goodness. Christian thinkers of later times were able to use his philosphy to express their faith. Aristotle thought of 'God' as being the 'First Cause' behind the universe. He taught that man shares his mind with God, and it alone is immortal. Such Greek thinkers went far in their search for God. They too helped to prepare the way for Christianity. But men cannot find God unless he makes himself known to them. Christianity brought the Gospel message, teaching which said that God had made himself known, once and for all, in Jesus of Nazareth.

As the times grew more troubled for the Greeks, their philosophers were more concerned with each individual. How could he or she live a good life in an evil world? How could he or she be happy in a life full of suffering? Four schools of philosophy grew up to answer these questions.

The CYNICS taught that the good life lay in freedom from desire, in retreat from the world, and in ignoring the 'good things' of life. SCEPTICS taught that, since nothing can be known for certain, there is no point in worrying about anything. EPICUREANS taught that men should 'live quietly', that the good life is simple and temperate. All desires should be avoided, since they destroyed peace of mind. The greatest evil was fear—especially fear of the gods and fear of death.

None of these schools of philosophy could become popular. Their appeal was to thinking men. Most people need to find a real purpose in life, not escape from it. They cannot ignore fear, especially fear of death, for it is part of our human instinct of self-preservation. They have desires and passions and worries that they cannot ignore. Men need to find a meaning in life and a hope for a future in death. Christianity gave both these in its Gospel.

The fourth school of philosophy was that of the STOICS. As we have seen, they won many noble Romans to their philosophy, and they too helped to prepare the way for Christianity. It was to supply what Stoicism lacked—a living, loving God.

FARM WORKERS

GRINDING CORN

Divisions in society

We can now begin to see how mixed society was in Roman times. Because it was so mixed there were many divisions. How did the Christian Church deal with these divisions?

There was, first, a great mix-up of religions. There were gods for the home, the city, the state, and, of course, for the empire in its divine ruler. There were secret Mystery Religions among the common folk, and followers of philosophy among the thinking and educated classes. The world was full of superstitions, magic, cults and philosophies, all competing with each other. Every race accepted this state of affairs, except for the Jews. With their belief in the one true God they could have nothing to do with all these pagan religions. Nor could they have anything to do with the evils that accompanied pagan worship. They alone served the true God. They had to keep themselves separate from all these other races—GENTILES (Latin 'gentes'—'peoples'). Thus, at the time, in religion, there was a division between Jews and Gentiles. The Christian Church began among Jews, but soon Gentiles were coming into it. Jews and Gentiles had to learn to live together in the Christian fellowship.

Another great division in the Roman world was between slaves and freemen. Roman conquests brought thousands of prisoners and most of them were made slaves. A rich man would have hundreds of slaves working on his estates. The emperor had thousands. There were no laws to protect slaves. They could be cruelly treated and put to death without question.

OIL PRESS

WINE PRESS

But they could also buy or be given their freedom, and the law allowed for this. Slaves could have great responsibilities in their masters' households. Freed slaves could rise to positions of great power. In the New Testament there are two Greek words, both concerned with slavery. Paul wrote of 'redemption' with God through faith in Jesus (Romans 3.24). The Greek word 'apolutrosis' means 'giving a slave his freedom'. Jesus himself said that he had come to give his life a 'ransom' for many (Mark 10.45). The Greek word here 'lutron' means 'the money paid to free a slave'. Being freed from slavery to a master was a symbol of being freed from the mastery of sin. Christians were not only free in the sight of God. When they entered the fellowship of the Church they joined a brotherhood in which there were no divisions. All were equal, united in love for God and for each other. Slaves and freemen were brothers in the family of God.

SLAVES RECEIVING THEIR FREEDOM

Two slaves are being freed in this relief showing the ceremony of 'manumission'. It dates from the first century C.E. One slave has already been freed and is shaking the hand of his former master. The other is kneeling on the ground, waiting for the touch of the magistrate's rod that will make him free. As part of the ceremony each has been given a 'pileus', the pointed skullcap that was the symbol of becoming a free man.

Some slaves became scholars and schoolmasters. They could achieve importance and fame as PEDAGOGUES—LEADERS OF CHILDREN. Paul, in his letters, sometimes speaks of the 'schoolmaster' (1 Corinthians 4. 15; Galatians 3. 24). The education of children in the Roman world was mainly in the basic subjects. Able students went on to study 'rhetoric'—that is, literature as well as the arts of speaking and writing. Such men, educated in Greek culture, were a class apart. A man's social position could be determined by his education. When Paul divided men into 'Greeks' and 'Barbarians' he could just as easily have said 'educated' and 'uneducated'. For education too divided society.

Wealth also made separate classes of rich and poor. Some could gain honour without wealth—for example, famous Greek athletes. Paul had seen the celebrated Games on the Isthmus of Corinth, and he likened the self-discipline of the athlete to that of the Christian (1 Corinthians 9. 24–26). But with wealth came all the good things of life. It brought fine houses, large estates, and many slaves. It provided feasts and banquets which became orgies of gluttony and drunkenness, with fine wines and rich delicacies from all over the world. Rich ladies spent hours with their slave-girls 'braiding their hair' (1 Timothy 2. 9). They adorned themselves with costly jewels and fine dress. Christians were told to be on their guard against such worldly folly and waste. Among them, in the family of the Church, wealth meant nothing. Rich and poor were brothers in the Christian Church.

Wrestlers

Gladiators

Boxers

Running

Jumping

Javelin-throwing

Discus-throwing

GAMES AND ATHLETICS

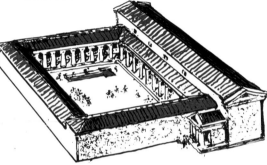

Amphitheatre
for gladiatorial
contests and wild
beast shows

Hippodrome
for horse and
chariot racing

Gymnasium
for athletic training

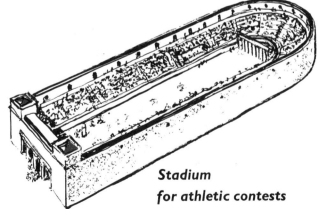

Stadium
for athletic contests

Thus people were divided in the Roman world by religion, by slavery, by education, by wealth. In the Christian Church these divisions meant nothing. They did not matter. All those who believed in Jesus as Lord were one family. Among Christians there were no divisions between Jews and Gentiles, between slaves and freemen, between educated and uneducated, between men and women, between rich and poor. When Paul said this he was simply describing life in the Christian Church (Galatians 3. 26–28; Colossians 3. 11). All members of the Church were united by their love for God their Father and by faith in Jesus their Lord.

The Jews

The Jews were a completely separate people in this Graeco-Roman world. They stood alone. Unlike those who followed Greek culture, they would not accept every religion and philosophy; and there were, at the time, so many different religions and cults and philosophies. Polytheism, belief in many gods, meant that any new religion could be accepted. Gods from other lands would be identified with Roman gods and then be included in the Roman Pantheon, as we saw. The Romans left people free to follow any religion, provided that it did not break the law. All peoples worshipped the same gods, under different names, and paid divine honours to the emperor. But Jews and Christians could do neither of these things.

The religion of the Jews was monotheism, belief in one God only. For them, no other gods existed; such 'gods' were simply wood and stone. Thus, it was quite impossible for them to identify their God with man-made gods. Nor could they ever worship a man, emperor or not.

There was another great difference between Jews and other peoples. Pagan religions had nothing to do with the way people lived. Men offered sacrifices, and performed the proper rites, to win the favour of their gods. The gods themselves, as men imagined them, were often immoral in their behaviour. They certainly had nothing to do with living a good life. In fact, many pagan religions actually encouraged immoral behaviour in their ceremonies and feasts. It was just the opposite with the Jews. They had come to know God as holy, just, and good. His worshippers must be the same. No amount of sacrifice could make up for evildoing. God had made known his moral demands in the sacred Law, and this was the heart of Jewish religion. To break the Law was to sin against God, and to be cut off from him. Thus, the religion of the Jews demanded good living. Pagan religions did not—they often encouraged evil living.

Again, the Jews believed that they were the 'chosen people' of God, called to fulfil his purpose. God was their ruler, not an earthly king. They must keep themselves distinct for God. They must hold on to their own separate identity. Such Jewish customs as keeping the sabbath, observing strict food laws, circumcising their male children, and marrying only among themselves, were part of their sacred Law. They kept the Jews a strictly separate people.

The Christian Church grew out of the Jewish tradition. The first Christians were all Jews, brought up in the Law. They had learnt not to worship with Gentiles. But what was to happen when Gentiles came to believe in Jesus and when the Spirit of Jesus came upon them? How could Jews live with Gentiles in the Church? This was to be a great problem for the Christian Church in its early days, as we shall see. It could only be solved by the love which bound all Christians together.

The Jewish Dispersion

In the sixth century B.C.E. the Jews had been taken away into exile in Babylon. When the Persians conquered Babylon, sixty years later, they were free to go back to Canaan. Not many did go back, for they had grown up in the lands of Babylonia. Their homes and livelihoods were there. They had gone into trade and commerce, and as merchants, they found their way to the great

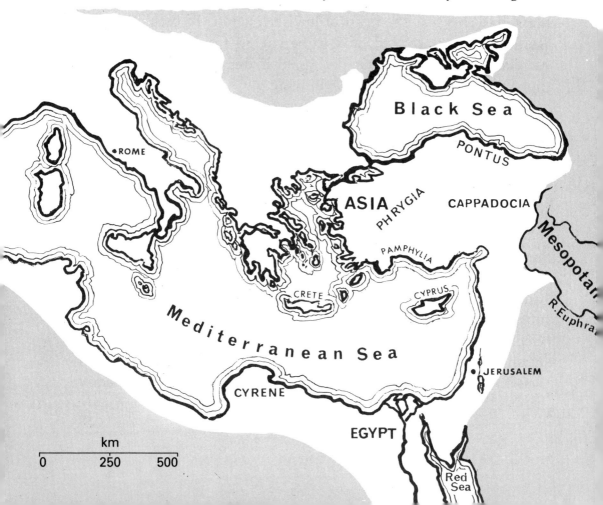

trading cities of the Mediterranean world. So began the DISPERSION (Greek 'diaspora'—'scattering') of the Jews among the nations. By the time the Christian Church was born, Jews were settled all over the Roman world. Only a minority of Jews lived in the Holy Land.

Jews were not particularly ill-treated by the Romans at that time. About 50 B.C.E. Julius Caesar had recognised them as a nation. This meant that they had special rights. They were free to worship their God, to live by their sacred Law, and to administer justice among themselves according to that Law. Special rights were granted to them, too. They did not have to worship the gods of Rome. They were permitted to pray *for* the emperor, and not *to* him. They did not have to do military service or to break their sabbath by attending law-courts.

The Jews were thus able to live their own life wherever they settled. There were a million Jews in Egypt, and another million in Asia Minor. There were Jewish colonies in Greece and in North Africa. All these Jews were called HELLENISTS, for they spoke the Greek language, they followed Greek customs, they used the Greek forms of their names. Their Scriptures had been translated

'Parthians, and Medes, and Elamites, and the dwellers in Mesopotamia, and in Judaea, and Cappadocia, in Pontus, and Asia, Phrygia, and Pamphylia, in Egypt, and in the parts of Libya about Cyrene, and strangers of Rome, Jews and proselytes, Crete and Arabians, we do hear them speak in our tongues the wonderful works of God.' Acts 2.9–11.

into Greek in the Septuagint. Hebrew, their traditional language, was only used in worship and that had to be translated into Greek during the service.

Yet these Hellenistic Jews of the Dispersion were dedicated to Judaism and lived by the Law. They traded with Gentiles, but they lived apart from them. They formed their own colony in any city where they settled. They were hard-working and law-abiding though living apart sometimes made them a target for pagan attacks. Their life was centred in the synagogue and in the worship of their God. They were not deeply affected by the Greek way of life, but they were more liberal than the Jews of the Holy Land. They were rather broader in their outlook, they did not distrust Gentiles as the Judaean Jews did. It is easy to understand why these Hellenistic Jews were more ready to listen to Christian preaching than the Jews of Judaea. When Peter first preached the Gospel in Jerusalem, on the Day of Pentecost, it was these Jewish pilgrims from abroad who listened to him. Seven deacons, chosen to help the apostles with their work, were all Hellenists. Christian missionary work began in Antioch, the great Hellenistic city of Syria, not in Jerusalem.

The Synagogue
Jews from abroad went as pilgrims to Jerusalem, if they could, for the great feasts—especially for the Passover. There they worshipped in the temple, offering sacrifices. But the local synagogue was the centre of their lives. SYNAGOGUE comes from a Greek word meaning MEETING-PLACE. Any ten male Jews could form a synagogue. In any city there might be a number of synagogues.

THE FOUNDATION-STONE OF A SYNAGOGUE

This stone was found in the old, lower city of Jerusalem in 1914. The Greek inscription reads:

THEODOTUS SON OF VETTENUS, PRIEST AND SYNAGOGUE-PRESIDENT, SON OF A SYNAGOGUE-PRESIDENT, AND GRANDSON OF A SYNAGOGUE-PRESIDENT, HAS BUILT THE SYNAGOGUE FOR THE READING OF THE LAW AND THE TEACHING OF THE COMMANDMENTS, AND (he has built) THE HOSTELRY AND THE CHAMBERS AND THE CISTERNS OF WATER IN ORDER TO PROVIDE LODGINGS FOR THOSE FROM ABROAD WHO NEED THEM – (the synagogue) WHICH HIS FATHERS AND THE ELDERS AND SIMONIDES HAD FOUNDED. (G.E. Wright)

This synagogue existed before the destruction of Jerusalem in C.E. 70. 'Son of Vettenus' means 'a freedman from the family of the Vetteni'. Thus, the family of Theodotus had been Jewish captives in Italy and had been given their freedom. This would have been a special synagogue for freed Jews from abroad. It is mentioned in Acts 6.9 – 'the synagogue of the Libertines' (Freedmen). Its members were bitter opponents of Stephen the deacon, who was stoned to death by a mob for his preaching of Jesus as the Messiah.

There would have been many such synagogues in Jerusalem alone. The Jews said that 480 synagogues had been destroyed by the Romans when they besieged and captured Jerusalem in C.E. 70.

There were thousands over the Roman empire, for wherever Jews settled new synagogues would arise. On the sabbath and on other special days Jews met at the synagogue for worship. They met there, too, at other times to settle the affairs of their community. By day, the synagogue was used as a school where Jewish boys learnt the Scriptures of their people.

The synagogue form of worship had grown up among the Jews in exile, when they could no longer sacrifice at Jerusalem. Its heart was the reading and teaching of the Law. There were readings from other writings, such as the scrolls of the Prophets, too. Hymns and prayers completed the service. Any Jew might be invited to read a lesson or to speak to the congregation, especially a visitor. Anyone could question the speaker. The worship of the synagogue kept Jews everywhere close to the Law. That was why the synagogue had two names—THE HOUSE OF PRAYER and THE HOUSE OF STUDY. In the synagogue service, and twice each day at home, the Jew recited the SHEMA ('Hear')—'Hear, O Israel, the Lord our God is one' (Deuteronomy 6. 4). It was the heart of his faith.

THE SYNAGOGUE SERVICE

The Shema

Deuteronomy 6.4–9;

Deuteronomy

11.13–21;

Numbers 15.37–41.

Prayers in praise of God

Giver of Light;

Lover of men;

Redeemer.

The Eighteen Benedictions (three examples)

Bless us, our Father, with the knowledge that cometh from thee,

And with intelligence and understanding from thy Law.

> Blessed art thou, O Lord,

> Gracious giver of knowledge.

Turn us to thyself again, O Lord, and so shall we return;

Renew our days as in the days of old.

> Blessed art thou, O Lord,

> Who hast pleasure in repentance.

Forgive us, our Father, for we have sinned against thee;

Wash away our transgressions from before thine eyes.

> Blessed art thou, O Lord,

> Who dost abundantly forgive.

Reading from the Law

– with translation from the Hebrew.

Reading from The Prophets

– with translation from the Hebrew.

Prayers

Psalms (hymns) for the day

The Blessing

The Lord bless thee and keep thee;

The Lord make his face to shine upon thee,

And be gracious unto thee;

The Lord lift up his countenance upon thee,

And give thee peace

(Numbers 6.24–26).

43

God-fearers

Not only Jews attended the synagogue service. Some Gentiles went there, too. They were called GOD-FEARERS, for they followed and practised the Jewish religion up to a point but without becoming Jews. They were high-minded Greeks and Romans, often well-educated, and devout. Three things attracted them to the religion of the Jews. It did not consist of crude sacrifices of animals, as in some religions, nor of strange initiation rites as in the Mystery Religions. It had, also, a pure belief in the one and only God, Creator and Lord of all things, and not the many gods and spirits and idols of pagan religions. It had, too, a pure moral law, teaching the good life, and not the immorality of pagan cults. Such a religion was different from all others, and it had a great appeal for thinking people. It taught a pure God, and a pure morality, and was itself a philosophy of life. Greek merchants and Roman officers, for example, would be attracted by it and follow its worship. We read of such a Roman soldier who had even built a synagogue for the Jews of Capernaum (Luke 7. 1–10).

The Jews did welcome converts to their religion—PROSELYTES, as they were called. But not many Gentiles became full Jews. To do that, they had to accept the Jewish Law completely, and there were parts of it which Gentiles found hard to accept. They did not like the custom of circumcision, or the Jewish food-laws or the strict sabbath laws of the Jews, or the traditional form of worship in the synagogue, where women seemed to have a smaller role. Many Gentiles became God-fearers. But few became proselytes.

Now the first Christian missionaries were, of course, Jews. When they came to a city they went straight to the Jewish quarter, as a matter of course. They joined in the synagogue worship and were naturally invited to speak. They preached that Jesus was the Messiah—the fulfilment of all the hopes of the Jews. Strict Jews found this preaching went against their most deeply held beliefs, and some became bitter enemies of Christian Jews. Even the more liberal Jews of the Dispersion did not find it easy to accept Jesus of Nazareth as the Christ. Paul was opposed by Jews all through his life. It was at the Greek city of Corinth that, after meeting the usual fierce reaction from the Jews, he said: 'from henceforth I will go to the Gentiles' (Acts 18. 6).

But the synagogue made a fine starting-point for the Christian preacher, wherever he went. Not many Jews came to faith in Jesus. But the God-fearers welcomed the Gospel of Christianity. It offered them all that they admired in Judaism, without the demands of the Jewish Law which they could not accept. They could become Christians by baptism in water, not by circumcision. There were no strict food-laws in Christianity, like the forbidding of pork; there was merely the rule of not eating meat that had been offered to idols. Instead of the restrictions of the Jewish sabbath, the Christians emphasised the joy of their Sunday. It was the first day of the week, a celebration of the resurrection of Jesus. Also, women and men together played a full part in the worship of God. It was for these reasons that God-fearers welcomed the Gospel of Christianity and entered the Church (Acts 13. 43; 16. 14–15).

Strict Jews could never be reconciled to the Christian faith. It was unthinkable to them to claim that the Messiah had come as this village carpenter, or to suggest that they were responsible for his death. Had Christianity remained in Jerusalem they might have put an end to it. But the Jewish Wars of C.E. 66–70 ended in the destruction of Jerusalem. By that time the Church had spread far and wide among Gentiles. Now it was free from the repeated attacks of strict Jews to become a worldwide Church.

MASADA

Masada was the fortress palace built by Herod the Great near the Dead Sea. After the fall of Jerusalem, it was occupied and held by the Zealots, an extreme Jewish sect. The Roman army encamped behind a 2 m siege wall, and built a ramp up which siege engines and rams were dragged. Masada fell in C.E. 73.

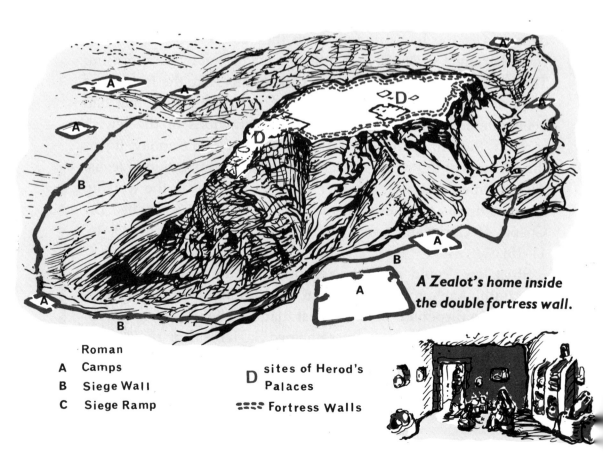

A Zealot's home inside the double fortress wall.

Roman
A Camps
B Siege Wall
C Siege Ramp
D sites of Herod's Palaces
≈≈≈ Fortress Walls

**Vespasian,
Emperor, C.E. 69–79**

**General of the
campaign**

THE ARCH OF TITUS AT ROME
SHOWING PLUNDER FROM JERUSALEM

Titus, the Roman general and later emperor, besieged and captured Jerusalem in C.E. 70. The Temple was destroyed and never rebuilt. This famous Arch, illustrating the triumphal procession of Titus on his return to Rome, still stands today. It shows Jewish prisoners in chains. Romans carry the booty with placards to describe each treasure. In this scene they carry the precious and sacred treasures from the Temple at Jerusalem – the golden table of the shewbread, silver trumpets, and the seven-branched golden candlestick.

The Holy Land

Our large maps of the Holy Land make us think of it as a large country. But it is, in fact, no bigger than Wales or Belgium. It is about 250 km from north to south, and 100 km wide from east to west. Its population in the first century would have been little more than a million people. Jerusalem was a city of about 100 000 people.

THE HOLY LAND IN THE TIME OF CHRIST

a scale comparision

km

0   100   200

Mediterranean Sea

GALILEE

SAMARIA

S. of Galilee

R. Jordan

JUDAEA

Dead Sea

But, however small the Holy Land was, its position made it very important. In early times it had been between the two great centres of ancient civilisation. One was the Nile Delta, the heart of the great kingdom of Egypt, to the south. The other, to the north and east, was the land of Mesopotamia—the LAND BETWEEN THE RIVERS, the Tigris and the Euphrates—which had been the homeland of several empires. The Holy Land was the corridor between these two kingdoms in Old Testament times.

Then came the rise of European empires to the west—first Greece and then Rome. Now the Holy Land became the meeting-place of three continents, Africa, Asia and Europe. There could have been no better birth-place for a new and universal religion. It was a religion that included men and women of all races and of all classes of society. It was a religion for the whole world. Jerusalem was like the hub of a wheel, the spokes radiating out to all lands. The Christian Church made its beginning from Jerusalem (Luke 24. 27). It could spread to east and west, to north and south, to 'the uttermost part of the earth' (Acts 1. 8).

'Preparation for the Gospel'

Romans, Greeks and Jews were the important peoples of the world into which Christianity came. All three helped in the spread of the Church. The Greeks prepared the way by their philosophy, their literature, and above all their language. The Romans prepared the way by their unified empire, their law and order, and peaceful travel by land and sea. The Jews had prepared the way by their widespread community so that in every land there were synagogues where Christian missionaries could find a ready-made audience for their preaching of the Gospel.

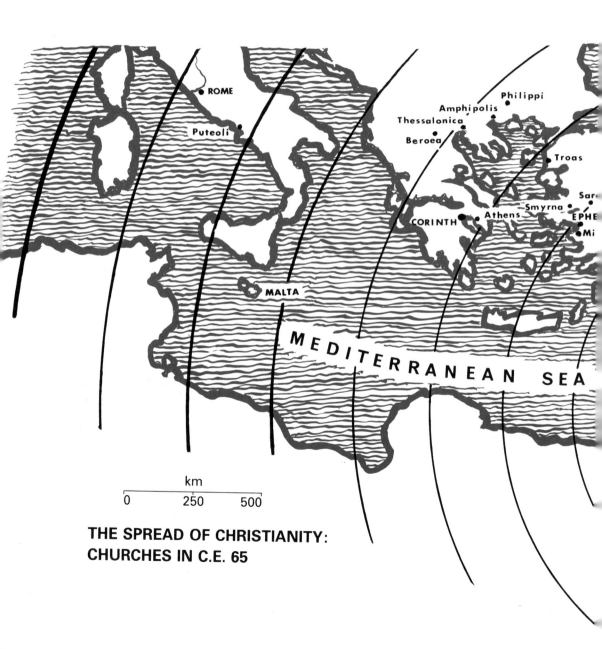

THE SPREAD OF CHRISTIANITY: CHURCHES IN C.E. 65

In such ways the world was ready for the spread of a new religion that could appeal to all peoples. Some Christians came to think that it had been divinely prepared. All that had happened was a 'Preparation for the Gospel'. The world had been made ready for the coming of the Christian Church.

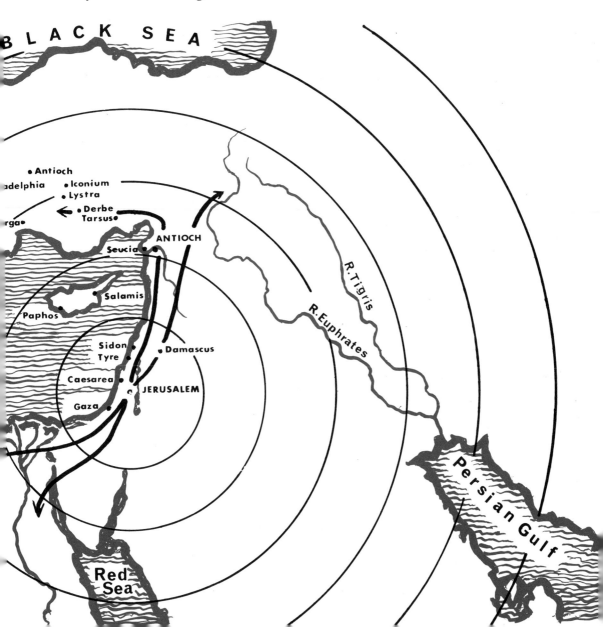

Bible references to find and read

Jesus is born under Augustus Caesar	Luke 2. 1–7.
Jesus' ministry begins under Tiberius	Luke 3. 1–3, 21–23.
Jesus Christ is Lord	Philippians 2. 11.
Peter recognises Jesus as the Christ	Mark 8. 27–30.
Paul a Roman citizen	Acts 22. 24–29.
Paul appeals to Caesar	Acts 25. 1–12.
Paul and Barnabas mistaken for gods	Acts 14. 8–18.
Stoic and Epicurean philosophers	Acts 17. 16–18.
Greeks and Barbarians	Romans 1. 14.
Athletes and Christians	1 Corinthians 9. 24–26.
All are one in the family of the Church	Galatians 3. 26–28 and Colossians 3. 11.
A Roman officer who was a God-fearer	Luke 7. 1–10.
God-fearers welcome the Gospel	Acts 13.42
Good News for all the world	Acts 1. 8.

To map

Make your own map of the Roman empire, showing its main cities and places where Jews were settled.

Some words to explain

Explain these words which have appeared in this chapter: Church; Lord; Christ; Pax Romana; Roman citizen; Asiarchs; polytheism; monotheism; lares and penates; Decapolis; Septuagint; Hellenism; Barbarians; philosophy; Gentiles; manumission; pedagogues; Pantheon; Dispersion; Hellenists; synagogue; proselytes; God-fearers.

To find out
Make lists of the four Cardinal Virtues and the three Theological
Virtues. Find out what each one means and describe its meaning.
If you have time, make up a story about each one.

To research
Use reference books to find out all you can about the gods of
Rome, many of which were Greek gods with a different name.
Draw some of these gods in a series of pictures, with a brief
description of each. Why was it that Jews and Christians would
have nothing to do with these gods?

To play a role
Imagine that you were a slave in Roman times, that your master
became a Christian and gave you your freedom. Describe what
happened.

To discuss
Imagine that you are members of a Christian church in Roman
times. Some of you will be Jews, some Gentiles, some 'Greeks',
some 'Barbarians', some slaves, some freemen, some rich, some
poor, some men, some women. Discuss why you have become
Christians, and what appeals to you in the church.

To debate
Some of you take the part of Stoics and others play the Christians.
Debate why it is that Stoics have many views in common with
Christians, yet do not accept their faith.

Words to define
The four main groups of Greek philosophers were Cynics, Sceptics, Epicureans and Stoics. We still use these words today, but they have rather different meanings. Find out what these terms mean today. How different are they from their original meaning?

A story to make up
Imagine yourself as a Roman citizen. Choose what you are—it may be a merchant, or banker, or missionary, or scholar, or a rich man fond of travelling. Describe a journey you make, the adventures you have, and how being a Roman citizen helps you on your travels.

To research
The whole class could join in a project on the Romans. Use reference books to find out all you can about their customs, clothes, food, dress, religions, and so on. Your stories, articles, maps, pictures and drawings can be used to make a class frieze or a class book.

To describe
Imagine that your family were Jews of the Dispersion and that you went with them on a pilgrimage to Jerusalem for the Passover Feast. Describe the differences that you found between the way you lived abroad and the way the Jews lived in Judaea.

To copy out and remember
Copy, in illuminated writing if you can, the fine Blessing in Numbers 6. 24–26 used in the synagogue service. That will help you to know it by heart.

See Acts 14.8–18

56

The Church among Jews

The Acts of the Apostles

The story of the beginnings of the Christian Church is recorded in the New Testament in the section called THE ACTS OF THE APOSTLES. It was written by a Gentile Christian, a Greek doctor called Luke (Greek 'Loukas', Latin 'Lucius'). He came from Philippi, a city of Macedonia in Greece. Luke was a well-educated man and a gifted writer. He wrote two of the books in the New Testament—almost a quarter of the whole text. This scholarly Greek chronicler played a very important role in handing down his account of events at this time as he saw them.

Luke wrote both his books for a man named 'Theophilus'. At the beginning of his first book, the Gospel of Luke, he addresses Theophilus as 'most excellent'—as we would say, 'Right Honourable'. This was an official title, so Luke may have written his books for a Greek or Roman official who was interested in Christianity. 'Theophilus' may have been a false name, to hide his real identity. Or it may have been the name which this official took when he became a Christian. In his Gospel, Luke wrote of all that Jesus 'began' to do and to teach. In his second book, the Acts of the Apostles, he recorded what he believed the Spirit of Jesus went on doing after his death. The early part of this book is concerned mainly with Peter, but most of the book is focused on Paul, the great Christian missionary. Paul made three missionary journeys.

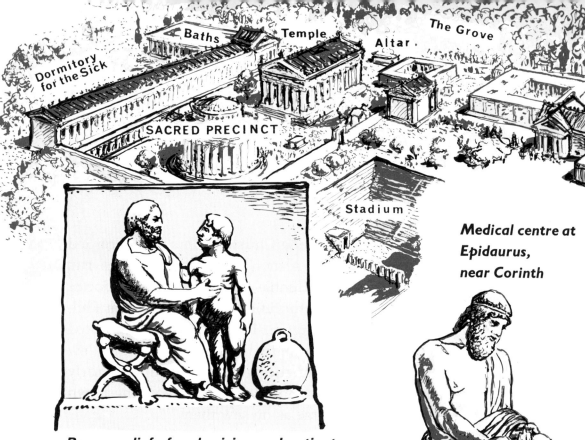

Baths

Temple

Altar

The Grove

Dormitory for the Sick

SACRED PRECINCT

Stadium

Medical centre at Epidaurus, near Corinth

Roman relief of a physician and patient

GREEK DOCTORS

Doctors were very highly regarded in the Roman world. Greek doctors were believed to be inspired by Asclepius, the god of healing. Near Corinth was a medical centre, dedicated to Asclepius, with temples, baths, gymnasium, theatre and stadium. Paul, in one of his letters, calls Luke the 'dear doctor' (Colossians 4.13–14).

A fifth century B.C.E. Greek statue of Asclepius (Asklepios) (son of Apollo and a mortal)

58

When he tells of Paul's second journey, Luke begins to write 'we' instead of 'he'. By now he was the travelling companion of Paul, for the Greek doctor had become a Christian. Paul suffered from some physical weakness, and Luke would have been of great help to him as his personal doctor. He would help, too, in spreading the Gospel of Jesus.

Luke wrote in a fine Greek literary style. He was at home in the Greek world, and knew little of the Jewish world. Christianity had transferred from being a Jewish sect to a Gentile church, so it is not surprising that Luke stresses the Jews' hostility to the Christian Church and speaks of the friendly welcome which Roman officials gave to Christian missionaries. In doing so, he gives us a striking picture of the Roman world. He describes, for example, how the men of Athens loved talk and argument; and how the greedy silversmiths of Ephesus rioted when Christians threatened their roaring trade in idols. He shows how men travelled in Roman times. On land they went by foot, by horse, or by chariot. On the sea, the coastal cargo ships went from port to port, hugging the land. The long sea voyage across the Mediterranean Sea was dangerous, especially as winter approached, and Luke gives us a vivid account of the shipwreck which he and Paul experienced on their journey to Rome. But, most important of all, Luke shows how the Christian Church grew and spread from distant Jerusalem to the capital city of the whole Roman empire; and how it spread from Jews to Gentiles.

We also learn much about the early years of the Church from the letters of Paul. All of them were written before Luke's account. They were sent to churches which Paul had founded. They dealt, mostly, with urgent matters which had arisen and they give us interesting glimpses of the growing Church. They add further detail to the story told by Luke.

The Gospel

What was the teaching which Christian missionaries were seeking to spread? We call it the GOSPEL, from the Old English words 'god spel' meaning GOOD NEWS. The Greek word was EVANGELLION, from which come our words EVANGEL and EVANGELIST. An EVANGELIST is therefore ONE WHO BRINGS GOOD NEWS.

We can best see what the Good News was from the speeches which Luke includes in The Acts of the Apostles. We find it in the addresses and sermons of the Christian preachers. It was the custom, in ancient times, for a writer to report speeches in his own words and style. But if not perhaps an exact record, they were based on what the speaker had said; and, of course, Luke had often heard Paul preaching the Good News.

We call this Good News the KERYGMA—the PROCLAMATION or ANNOUNCEMENT. Its claims were

(1) The Jewish Scriptures had been fulfilled and the new age, promised by the prophets, had come.

(2) It had come in Jesus who was the long-promised Messiah. He had been put to death on the cross, and raised up by God. The apostles were bearing witness to his life and death and rising again.

(3) Because the Messiah had come, the Spirit of God was now at work in his Church.

(4) The presence of the Spirit of Jesus in his Church was clear proof that the new age had come.

(5) Those who heard this proclamation should change their lives, believe in Jesus, be baptised into his Church, and so receive the power of his Spirit.

All the preaching of Christian missionaries was based on these beliefs. They could be summed up in a short and simple CREED—A

STATEMENT OF BELIEF (Latin 'credo'—'I believe'). The first creed we find was simply JESUS CHRIST IS LORD. Another creed, a little later, was I BELIEVE THAT JESUS CHRIST IS THE SON OF GOD. This was the heart of the Christian faith.

THE GOSPEL IN THE CREED

This is called the Apostles' Creed, for it sums up their teaching. The earliest written record of it dates from about C.E. 400, so that it must be much earlier than that. It is still today the Creed of the Christian Churches.

I believe

In God the Father Almighty,

Maker of heaven and earth;

And in Jesus Christ

His only Son our Lord,

Who was conceived by the Holy Ghost,

Born of the Virgin Mary,

Suffered under Pontius Pilate,

Was crucified, dead and buried,

He descended into hell;

The third day he rose again from the dead,

He ascended into heaven,

And sitteth on the right hand of God the Father Almighty;

From thence he shall come to judge the quick and the dead.

I believe in the Holy Ghost;

The holy catholic Church;

The communion of saints;

The forgiveness of sins;

The resurrection of the body,

And the life everlasting.

Amen.

The Day of Pentecost

After Jesus had been crucified, his followers still met together in an 'upper room'. This was the 'guest-chamber', built on the flat roof of better houses and approached by an outside stone stairway. The disciples would go on meeting at the house of Mark's mother, where the Last Supper had been held, and this would be their headquarters. There were about 120 disciples altogether, all of them from Galilee. They included the apostles, Mary the mother of Jesus, and at least one of his brothers, James, who was to become a leader of the church at Jerusalem.

Judas Iscariot had committed suicide in remorse for having betrayed Jesus. Peter proposed that another disciple should be chosen to fill the place of Judas and so to make up the band of twelve. This was a symbolic number to the Jews. In ancient times there had been twelve 'founders' of the Twelve Tribes of the Jews, which had grown from the twelve sons of Jacob. Jesus had chosen twelve apostles, a symbol that they were to be the twelve heads of the New Israel, the Christian Church. The group of disciples cast lots to choose a successor to Judas. This was a common way of seeking a sign, in those times, and the result was believed to show the divine will. A disciple named Matthias was chosen in this way to make up the twelve.

62

It was on the Day of Pentecost that the disciples, gathered in the upper room, had the wonderful experience which made this day the birthday of the Church. PENTECOST comes from a Greek word meaning FIFTIETH, for this Feast, or festival, came fifty days after the beginning of the Passover Feast. Its Hebrew name was SHAVUOT, meaning WEEKS. From this came another title for the Feast—FEAST OF WEEKS—forty-nine days (seven weeks) after the Passover. Pentecost, which came in May or June, was the Harvest Festival of the new wheat. Worshippers offered loaves of bread at the Temple. It was one of the three great pilgrim festivals of the Jewish year which all Jews had to keep. Jews who lived in Judaea went to the Temple at Jerusalem, if they could. Those Jews of the Dispersion who lived in other lands came as pilgrims. Pentecost had an even greater significance than Harvest Festival. It had become the festival of the giving of the sacred Law to Moses on Mount Sinai, and nothing was more precious to Jews than the Law of God. No wonder that Jerusalem was crowded with Jews from all over the world for the great Day of Pentecost.

CHRISTIAN SYMBOLS OF THE HOLY SPIRIT

The Descending Dove

The traditional symbol, based on the story of the baptism of Jesus, Luke 3.21–22.

The sevenfold flame

A symbol of tongues of fire, based on the story of the Day of Pentecost, Acts 2.1–4.

The seven lamps

Symbols of the seven gifts of the Spirit: Wisdom; Understanding; Counsel; Ghostly Strength; Knowledge; True godliness; Holy fear (see Isaiah 11.2).

The Holy Spirit

It was on that day that the Spirit of God came upon the disciples of Jesus. The Jewish people had long believed in the Spirit. It was God's power at work in the world—in creation, in giving life, in giving special talents, and in the inspiration of his messengers the prophets. Jews expressed the Spirit of God as BREATH or WIND. Both the Hebrew word 'ruach' and the Greek word 'pneuma' mean 'spirit' or 'wind'. A man filled with the 'breath' of God is INSPIRED, meaning BREATHED INTO. The winds were God's messengers, and fire was another symbol of his burning power. This helps us to understand Luke's account of what happened on that day. He says that the disciples in the upper room felt the sensation of a 'rushing mighty wind' and of 'fire'. Luke had not been there. He would get the story from the Jewish Christians who had been present. Naturally they used

Jewish symbols—*like* wind and fire (but not *actually* wind and fire)—to convey the wonderful sensation of being inspired by the power of God.

This power is known by Christians as the HOLY GHOST. GHOST comes from the Old English word 'gast'. It means exactly the same as SPIRIT, which comes from the Latin word 'spiritus'. Hence the expression 'to give up the ghost', meaning 'to die'. Thus 'Holy Ghost' and 'Holy Spirit' have exactly the same meaning. Both stand for the power or inspiration of God.

The disciples, after their astonishing experience, rushed down from the upper room into the street. Some bystanders thought that they must be drunk. But that was impossible, for it was early and no Jew drank wine before the hour of morning prayer. A crowd quickly gathered in the street, astonished to hear the disciples 'speaking with tongues'. This 'gift of tongues' (Greek: 'glossolalia') has often resulted from strong religious experience. In ancient times, the strange sounds made by an inspired man were regarded as a clear sign that a spirit was within him, speaking through him. To Christians this was a 'gift of the Holy Spirit'. Paul had this gift himself, but he wrote that there were much more important gifts of the Spirit—above all, love.

The crowd which gathered was made up of Jewish pilgrims from all over the world. The list mentions first the Jews from Parthia, Media, Elam and Mesopotamia. All these lands were outside the Roman Empire. Then follows a list of provinces of the Roman Empire from which the rest of the crowd had come. The provinces of Cappadocia, Pontus, Asia, Phrygia and Pamphylia were in the area of Asia Minor. There were Jews present, too, from Egypt and from Cyrene in North Africa. From Rome came

Jews whose fathers would have been taken to Italy as captives. Others came from the island of Crete. Those from Arabia lived in the kingdom of the cultured Nabatean people. Thus, the Jews who heard the Good News preached that day came from all lands between Italy in the west to almost the borders of India in the east. (See the map on pages 38–39).

The Parousia

Peter preached the Gospel to the crowd that had gathered. He proclaimed Jesus as the Messiah, cruelly put to death by men and raised up by God. The outpouring of the Spirit of God was the proof of his announcement. Peter spoke with urgency, as did all the early Christian preachers, for they believed that the end of the world was at hand. Jesus would shortly come again to earth to set up his kingdom. The Greek word for this belief is PAROUSIA. It means BEING NEAR and so APPEARANCE or SUDDEN ARRIVAL. Jesus would suddenly appear, coming on the clouds of heaven, in power and in glory.

How did this belief arise? It came, originally, from Jewish hopes of a Messiah. The prophets had taught that God would reveal himself in history. The great leader he would send to his people would come from the family of David. But this hope had not been realised. The history of the Jews grew more troubled, not better. They were conquered by one empire after another. Some Jews despaired of God revealing himself in history. They thought more and more of a heavenly deliverer, coming with great signs and wonders. They described this great climax in visions and revelations. We call these writings APOCALYPTIC, from a Greek word meaning TO UNCOVER. They were very popular among the Jews during the two centuries before the coming of Jesus. They were being persecuted for their religion, and these writings, telling how God would reveal himself in great triumph, gave them great encouragement.

These ideas became linked with Jesus. We find examples of apocalyptic writings in the Gospels, as well as in the Book of Revelation. Jesus had promised his disciples that he would be with them. He would leave them, but he would return to them in his Spirit (John 14. 18–24 and 16. 16–22). This return of Jesus became linked with apocalyptic ideas. Jesus would return with great signs and wonders. Jesus had called himself the 'Son of Man'. One picture of the Son of Man had been given in the Book of Daniel, an apocalyptic book of the Old Testament. He had been described there as 'coming on the clouds of heaven' (Daniel 7. 13–14). Thus Jesus would soon return to earth, suddenly, and in power and glory. The world would end and God's kingdom would be established.

This belief was strong among the first Christians. It made their preaching urgent. It shaped their lives, too, as we shall see. But in the later letters of Paul we can see this belief beginning to fade. Christians came to realise that Jesus had already returned in his Spirit. He was present in their hearts and in his Church.

The Church is born
After Peter had proclaimed the Good News on that Day of Pentecost, his hearers asked him what they must do. Peter called on them to 'repent'—to change their minds, to turn their backs upon

the past, and to start a new life. Then, believing and repenting, they could enter the Church by baptism. The Jews had been using this custom before the coming of Jesus. They baptised Gentiles who wished to become proselytes, to become full Jews. John the Baptist had used this practice as a symbol of purifying for those who responded to his teaching and desired to prepare themselves for the coming of the Messiah whom he announced. The apostles of Jesus used baptism during his ministry (John 4. 1–2). They naturally went on using it as the means of entering the Church of Jesus.

Believers were baptised in LIVING, that is, in RUNNING water. They were baptised by 'total immersion'—going down into the water and being completely covered by it. This method of baptism has always been suitable in hot countries, out in the open air. We can see why Paul described baptism as a symbol of sharing the death and resurrection of Jesus (Romans 6. 3–4). Believers went down into the water and came up out of it with new life. They had washed away the old life in the purifying waters of baptism. Baptism could be likened, too, to putting on a new garment. A Christian, through his baptism, 'put on' Christ.

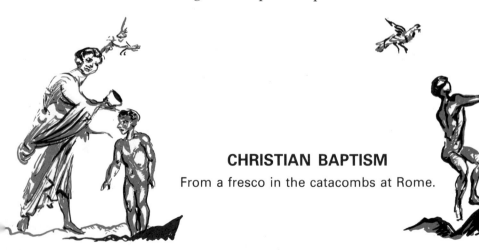

CHRISTIAN BAPTISM
From a fresco in the catacombs at Rome.

Baptism had two parts. The first was immersion in water to symbolise the washing away of the 'old' man, the old life. Then followed the 'laying on of hands' on the head of the believer—a symbol of receiving the power of the Spirit to live a new life. That is why the Spirit was called the PARACLETE, from a Greek word meaning ONE WHO AIDS. Another term for the Spirit is COMFORTER, from a Latin word meaning ONE WHO STRENGTHENS.

We read that 3000 people were baptised on the Day of Pentecost. It was the birthday of the Christian Church, and it has been kept as the festival of the Holy Spirit ever since. Naturally it became a favourite day for baptism. As the custom was to wear white for baptism, this festival of the Holy Spirit became known as WHITE SUNDAY. From it we get our word WHITSUNDAY.

Life in the Church

The first Christians at Jerusalem still joined in the Jewish worship at the Temple. But they lived together in a brotherhood among themselves, meeting in each other's houses. They shared in a common meal called the AGAPE or LOVE-FEAST. It was a symbol of their love for each other as members of the family of Jesus. The most important part of the meal was the remembrance of the Last Supper. They shared bread and wine, as Jesus had bidden them. This united them with Jesus their Lord, so that they shared in his life. For Jesus had used the bread as a symbol of his body, and the wine as a symbol of his blood, to be given for men. They were symbols of the giving of his life to make a New Testament (or covenant) between men and God.

69

CHRISTIANS SHARING BREAD AND WINE

From a fresco in the catacombs at Rome

Christians also expressed their love for each other in sharing. Giving had always been a part of Jewish religion. It was a symbol of recognising that everything came from God. It was necessary, too, to give for the upkeep of the worship of Temple and synagogue. It was also a duty to fellow-Jews, especially to those in need. All Jews regarded it as a sacred duty to give ALMS—an old English word which came from a Greek word meaning SHOWING SYMPATHY.

The Christian Church began among a small group of Jews. In their joy and enthusiasm they gave all their possessions to the apostles to be shared out. Those who owned houses or fields or valuables sold them, and gave the proceeds to the Church. No Christian regarded anything as his own property. Everything was put into the common pool for the leaders to share out according to need. This was a kind of COMMUNISM—in the sense of having all things in common, and no private property. It is the way monks live together in a monastery. It is the way we live together in our homes. Of course, this true sharing is always based on love. Political 'communism', in the world today, is something based on a quite different set of ideas. Real sharing must always be done freely, not ordered by laws, for it is inspired by love.

This spontaneous sharing, among the first Christians at Jerusalem, could not last. They believed, as we have seen, that Jesus would soon return to earth, and therefore they did not need to bother about the future. But life had to go on, and Christians could not give without earning. This style of community living ended, but giving and sharing did not end. New ways were found of helping those in need. Collections were made at meetings of the Church, and each member gave what he could. Christians thought of themselves as 'stewards' of their possessions, as they still do. Part of all they earned must be given to God in the work of his Church.

Jewish opposition

The power of the Spirit was strong among the early Christians. One expression of it, as we saw, was 'speaking with tongues'. Another was the gift of healing. Luke records how Peter healed a lame man. He had been lame from birth, and he was laid each day outside the Gate Beautiful—one of the eight gates leading to the Temple—to collect alms. Peter and John were on their way to the Temple for the evening service. In his excitement at being able to walk, the healed man made a great commotion. A crowd soon gathered in Solomon's Porch, a cloister in the Temple Courts. Peter and John preached the Good News to them, but they were interrupted by the Temple guards, seized, and put in custody for the night.

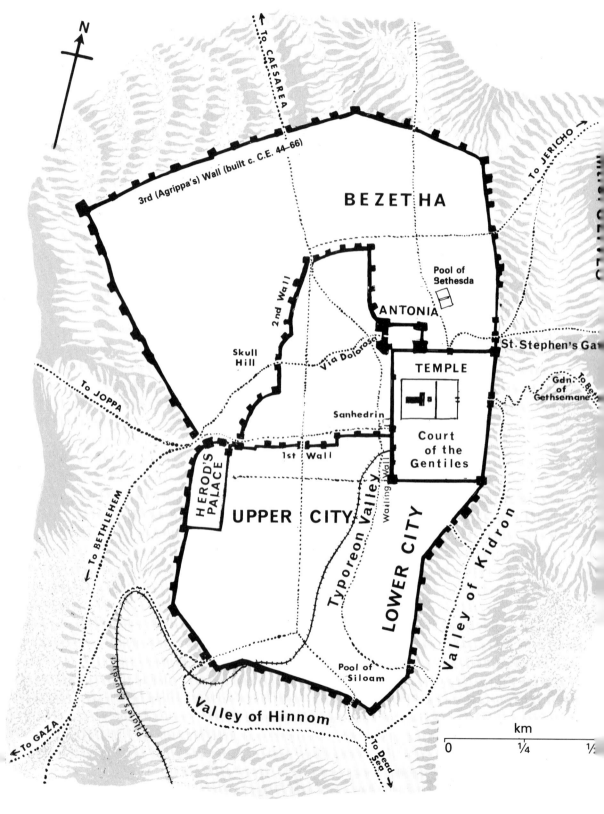

N

To CAESAREA

3rd (Agrippa's) Wall (built c. C.E. 44–66)

BEZETHA

Pool of
Bethesda

ANTONIA

2nd Wall

Skull
Hill

Via Dolorosa

St. Stephen's Gate

To JOPPA

Sanhedrin

TEMPLE

Court
of the
Gentiles

Gdn.
of
Gethsemane

To Bethany

HEROD'S
PALACE

1st Wall

UPPER CITY

Wailing Wall

Typoreon Valley

LOWER CITY

Valley of Kidron

To GAZA

To BETHLEHEM

Pilate's Aqueduct

Pool of
Siloam

Valley of Hinnom

To Dead
Sea

To JERICHO

Mt. of OLIVES

km

0   ¼   ½

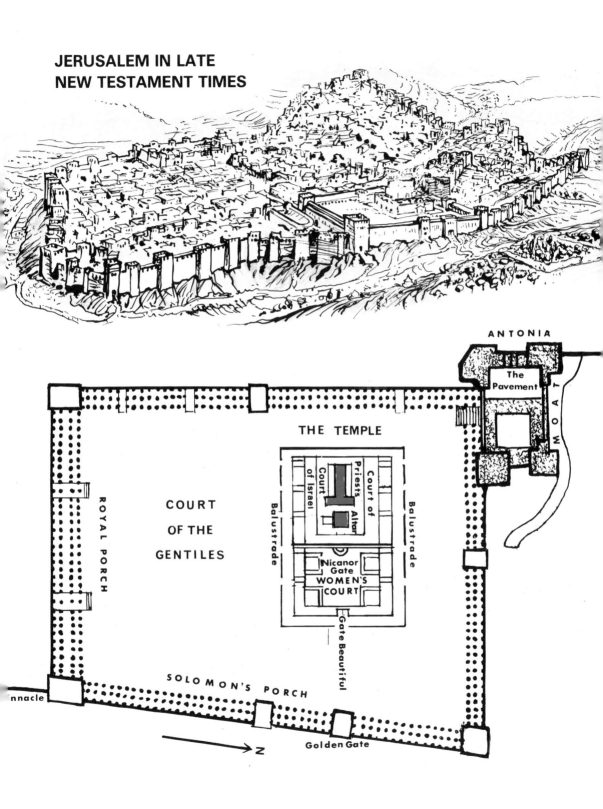

JERUSALEM IN LATE NEW TESTAMENT TIMES

ANTONIA

The Pavement

M O A T

THE TEMPLE

ROYAL PORCH

COURT OF THE GENTILES

Balustrade

Court of Israel

Court of Priest's

Altar

Balustrade

Nicanor Gate

WOMEN'S COURT

Gate Beautiful

SOLOMON'S PORCH

innacle

N

Golden Gate

The guards had been sent by the SADDUCEES—the aristocratic, priestly families of Jerusalem who controlled the Temple. They were few in number but they were a rich and powerful group. They kept well in with the Romans in order to preserve what independence they had, and the power they inherited. They were unpopular with the people, for they had nothing in common with them and despised them. They made their wealth from the Temple tax, paid by all Jews both at home and abroad. They were quick to see any threat to their vested interest in the Temple. Already they had taken a leading part in the campaign against Jesus. Now they were faced with his disciples. Peter and John had addressed the people without having any authority to do so. They had preached that Jesus of Nazareth, executed as a criminal, was the Messiah. They had caused a public sensation by healing a man who had been lame from birth. Such activities must be stopped at once.

The next day the SANHEDRIN was summoned. This was the COUNCIL or 'Parliament' of the Jews, recognised officially by the Romans. It had 71 members, with the high priest as chairman. Sadducees were leading members of it, together with Scribes, teachers of the Law, and Pharisees. The PHARISEES were a lay group of devout men who were opponents of the Sadducees. The Sadducees were very conservative in their outlook, keeping strictly to the old written Law. The Pharisees developed unwritten teachings from the Law, so as to apply it to new conditions of life and to cover every part of it. They also developed new customs in worship, new religious festivals, the custom of baptising proselytes, the hope of the Messiah, and new beliefs in angels and spirits and in resurrection. The Sadducees rejected all these things.

Sanhedrin

Pharisee **High Priest** **Sadducee**

Jesus and his followers represented a theological challenge to the Jewish faith. The Sadducees might well have felt that Jesus could upset the delicate balance of their relationship with the Romans. Both Pharisees and Sadducees, however, were united in their opposition to the new teaching that arose after Jesus' death. They threatened Peter and John before letting them go, and hoped to frighten them into silence. But they did not succeed.

The Church among 'Hebrews'

The new Christian society grew steadily in numbers through the preaching of the apostles. The majority of the first Christians, beginning with the apostles and disciples of Jesus, were HEBREWS—that is, Jews brought up in Judaea who spoke the Aramaic language and used in their worship the old Hebrew language of their people. Daily in Solomon's Porch they preached Jesus to their fellow Jews. Their popularity grew through their preaching and healing. But so did the suspicions of the Sadducees. The apostles were again arrested and brought before the Council. They were charged with 'filling Jerusalem' with their teaching after they had been warned not to do so. Peter answered: 'We must obey God, not men.' He went on to speak of Jesus as the Messiah to the members of the Council. They were so angered that they began to consider how they could get rid of these dangerous fanatics.

It was then that a famous rabbi named Gamaliel swayed the Council. He was the grandson of another great rabbi, named Hillel, the originator of the liberal view among the Pharisees. They stood for tolerance in interpreting the Law, and Gamaliel was now their leader. He quoted recent cases of other strange teachers to the Council. They had been quickly put down by the Roman authorities, and their followers had been easily dispersed. Their beliefs and teachings had come to nothing. The best policy, Gamaliel advised, was to wait and see—not to start a persecution. If this new teaching was just another craze it would soon wither and die, too. But if, on the other hand, it had come from God then the Council would be going against God if they attacked it. The members of the Council followed the wise advice of Gamaliel. The apostles were beaten, ordered once more not to preach in the name of Jesus, and then released.

The Church among 'Hellenists'

From the very beginning, on the Day of Pentecost, the Good News was heard by Jews from abroad. We call them HELLENISTS, a word that comes from 'Hellenism', the term for 'Greek culture' ('Hellas'—'Greece'). For Jews in other lands spoke the Greek language, read the Jewish Scriptures in Greek, and followed Greek

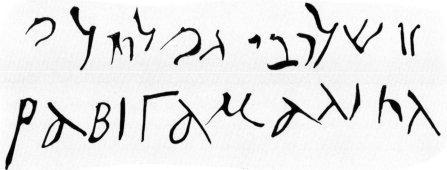

Inscription in Hebrew on the Tomb of Gamaliel. The words 'Rabbi Gamaliel' are repeated in Greek.

customs in their daily lives. Many came to Jerusalm as pilgrims; some of them settled in the city. The Jews of Judaea, proud of living in the Holy Land, were suspicious of Jews from abroad, and were uncertain as to how strict they were in their interpretation of the Law.

Hellenists, as well as Hebrews, were attracted by Christianity and baptised into the Church. Differences arose between them over the care and help of those in need. The Hellenists began to complain that their poor widows were not getting their fair share. The apostles called a meeting of all the believers. They proposed that seven good men, full of the Spirit, should be chosen to help them in the practical tasks of caring for the needy. Seven was a symbolic number to Jews. These seven helpers were called DEACONS or SERVANTS of the Church. Everyone agreed, and seven good members were selected. All of them were Hellenists, Greek-speaking Jews from abroad.

The seven deacons did not merely do practical tasks. Naturally they taught and preached, too. One of them was Stephen, a man of great eloquence and spirit. He spoke with great conviction in the synagogues of the Hellenists. He preached Jesus to Jews from Cyrene in Africa, from Alexandria in Egypt, and from the eastern provinces of Cilicia and Asia. Some of them grew jealous of Stephen's success and they became his enemies. They bribed false witnesses to accuse him of blasphemy, and Stephen was brought before the Council. He had no fear and made no attempt to defend himself. He proclaimed his faith with great conviction. God, he said, had no need of a temple to dwell in. He claimed that the Jews had always rejected him, killed his prophets, and broken his Law. Now they had murdered the Messiah himself. The members of the Council could stand no more. There was no chance to give a ruling. They broke into an uproar and, mad with rage, thrust Stephen out through the city gate and stoned him to death. But this act of mob violence broke Roman law, for the Council was not allowed to put anyone to death. Only the Roman procurator could do that. The stoning of Stephen was only possible because of political unrest and disorder at the time.

Stephen was the first Christian MARTYR or WITNESS, bearing witness to his faith by dying for it. His martyrdom was to have great effects upon the Church, for a Jew from Cilicia stood by, watching him die. He was Saul of Tarsus, a student of the great rabbi Gamaliel. He had been brought up as a Pharisee and he was dedicated to the Law. To him, the preaching of Jesus as the Messiah was blasphemy. The followers of Jesus were heretics. He gladly stood by during the stoning of Stephen. But it was an experience that he could never forget. It was to change his whole life. It turned Saul of Tarsus into Paul, the great Christian missionary.

**ST. STEPHEN'S GATE,
JERUSALEM TODAY**

It was built in the sixteenth century C.E.

The Church among Samaritans

The stoning of Stephen was a turning-point for Christians. Until then they had been regarded simply as a sect of Jews. Now they were a separate group of heretics, whose beliefs were seen to be contrary to Judaism. Now began a fierce persecution of the Christians—NAZARENES, as they were known. Those, like the apostles, who were from Judaea were not attacked. The persecution was against Hellenists who, like Stephen, put their faith in Jesus rather than in the Temple and the Law. The seven deacons were the leaders of the Hellenists, and they were marked men. Already Stephen had been murdered. The others were in danger, too.

One of them, named Philip, fled to Samaria. Naturally he preached the Gospel to the Samaritans. As a Jew from abroad,

80

Philip did not share the hatred of the Jews of Judaea for the Samaritans. They despised the Samaritans, and even though some of them came from Jewish stock and followed Jewish religion, there was a traditional enmity between the Jews and the Samaritans, dating back many hundreds of years. They would have nothing to do with the Samaritan people. This could well make Samaritan territory an unsafe place for Jewish travellers. They would have been very unlikely to go near the city of Samaria.

Caesar Augustus had given it to Herod the Great in 30 B.C.E. Herod had rebuilt the city and renamed it in honour of Augustus. He called it SEBASTE, from 'sebastos', the Greek form of 'Augustus'; and still today the village of Sebastiyeh bears this name. Herod needed a strong city there to help to control the countryside. Archaeologists have .ound that the walls were over a kilometre long, and strengthened with sturdy towers. Herod built a fine pagan temple in honour of Augustus, and made Samaria into a typical Greek city. It had its Forum, a large open shopping-centre. Its stadium was built according to the standard size of the stadium in Greece where the Olympic Games were held, over 180 m long and 58 m wide. Herod the Great loved the Greek games and made large contributions to their funds. He completed his work at Samaria by settling 6000 of his troops there. Samaria was now a completely Greek city—that is, a pagan city to Jews. Yet it was there that Philip went and preached Christianity.

Philip won believers by his preaching and he baptised them into the Church. When the apostles at Jerusalem heard of this they sent Peter and John to Samaria. They completed the baptism of the Samaritan believers by the 'laying on of hands'. They too had the experience of the Spirit of God coming upon them.

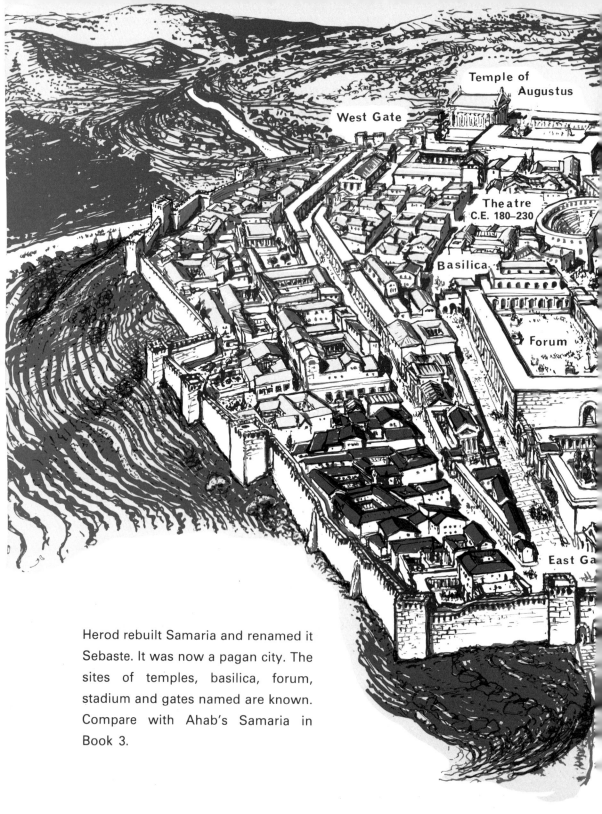

West Gate

Temple of Augustus

Theatre
C.E. 180–230

Basilica

Forum

East Ga

Herod rebuilt Samaria and renamed it
Sebaste. It was now a pagan city. The
sites of temples, basilica, forum,
stadium and gates named are known.
Compare with Ahab's Samaria in
Book 3.

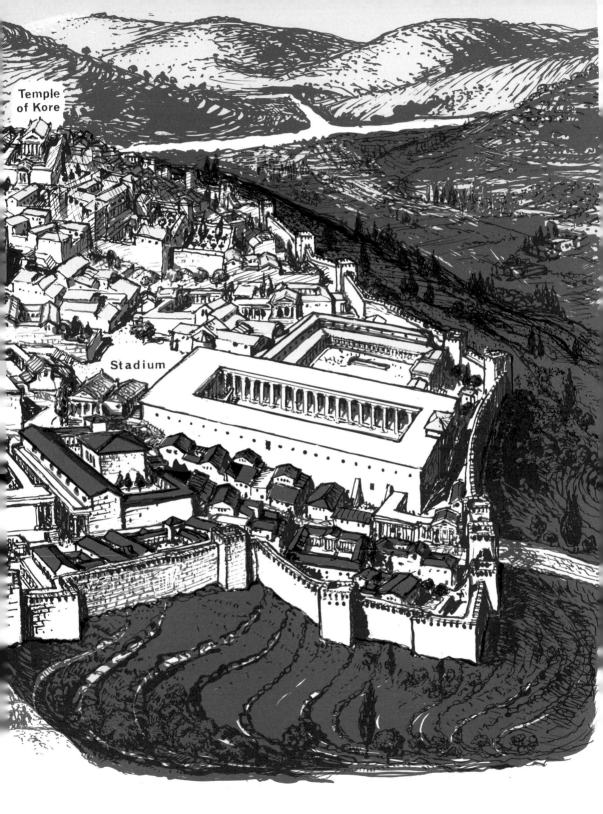

Temple
of Kore

Stadium

The Church on the Coast

We know Philip the deacon as PHILIP THE EVANGELIST or BEARER OF GOOD NEWS. That is to distinguish him from Philip the apostle. After his stay at Samaria, he made his way towards the coastal plain along by the Mediterranean Sea. The next story of him tells how he was travelling along the road from Jerusalem to Gaza, by the sea. Gaza was a great trading centre, for it was the crossroads between four great caravan routes. One went south to Arabia, another south-west to Egypt, a third south-east to Edom, and a fourth was the main route to the north, along the coastal plain and up to Damascus. It is from the fine textiles of Gaza that we get our word 'gauze'.

Philip met a caravan on the road to Gaza. It belonged to an important official from Ethiopia, in Africa, who was on his way back home from Jerusalem. He was the treasurer of the Candace, as the queen of Ethiopia was known, and a well-educated nobleman. He was a God-fearer, and he may have been to Jerusalem for the Feast of Tabernacles. For Philip found him reading aloud the lesson for that Feast—the description of the Suffering Servant of God in Isaiah 53. Philip gladly agreed to explain the passage to him. He showed the African how Jesus, in his suffering and death, had fulfilled the prophecy of the Suffering Servant who, though innocent himself, died for others. The Ethiopian believed and Philip gladly baptised him at a roadside oasis.

Philip went on towards the coast. He came to Azotus, the ancient city of the Philistines known as Ashdod. Then he journeyed to Joppa, on the coast, and finally to Caesarea where he settled. Luke would have heard these stories from Philip himself, for he and Paul stayed at Philip's home at Caesarea on their way

km
0   25   50

**THE CHURCH SPREADS
OUT FROM JERUSALEM
THROUGH PHILIP AND
PETER**

ROMAN PROVINCE OF SYRIA

GALILEE

Sea of Galilee

DECAPOLIS

CAESAREA

SAMARIA

Samaria
(Sebaste)

PERAEA

Joppa

Lydda

JERUSALEM

Azotus
(Ashdod)

Dead Sea

JUDAEA

Gaza

IDUMAEA

to Jerusalem (Acts 21. 8–15). Paul was arrested at Jerusalem and he was imprisoned in the governor's residence at Caesarea for two years. Luke was with him, but he was free to come and go. He would have spent much time with Philip, during those two years, gathering memories and records to include in the Acts.

The work of Philip shows how the Church was beginning to spread outwards from Jerusalem. It was spreading, too, to other peoples. Philip himself had baptised Samaritans and an African. He had preached and baptised along the coast. Like Stephen, he had begun to see that Jesus was not only the Messiah of one people. He welcomed men of all nations into his Church. Now came a further development of the Church. It concerns Peter, and it takes us to the Mediterranean Coast—to the towns of Caesarea and Joppa.

The Church at Caesarea

There was no natural, deep-water harbour along the coast of the Holy Land. Herod the Great had therefore spent twelve years building a good, artificial seaport for his kingdom. He named it CAESAREA, in honour of his patron, the emperor Augustus. So fine was the city he built that it became the seat of the Roman

CAESAREA, A RECONSTRUCTION
Caesarea harbour shown on a coin, 6 B.C.E. to C.E. 4

Procurators and the chief city of Judaea. Herod's engineers made an artificial harbour, 37 mm deep, with a mole and breakwater of solid stone. The city included a temple in honour of Augustus, a theatre for Greek plays and musical performances, an open forum surrounded by shops, and a stadium. Its amphitheatre enclosed an oval even larger than that in the Colosseum at Rome—90 m long and 60 m wide. Here gladiators fought with wild beasts, just as they did in Rome. The governor's residence was the headquarters of Roman troops. Stationed there, at this time, was the Italian cohort, a regiment of 500 foot soldiers with a tribune in charge. One of its centurions was a God-fearer named Cornelius.

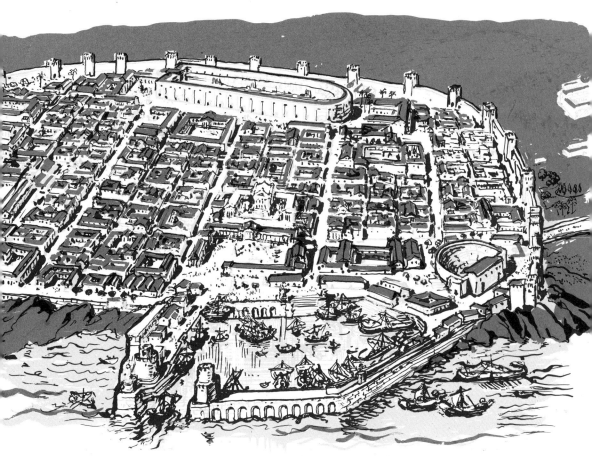

ROMAN INSCRIPTION FROM CAESAREA

This stone was found in 1961 in the ruins of the theatre at Caesarea, built by Herod the Great. It has an inscription in Latin, the language of the Romans, which includes the name of Pontius Pilate. It is the first evidence found referring to Pilate, Procurator of Judaea from C.E. 26–36, who sentenced Jesus to the cross.

Luke relates how Cornelius became a Christian through Peter the apostle. Peter was staying at Joppa, 50 km down the coast from Caesarea. Joppa was the only natural harbour on the coast, but it had no depth of water. Only coastal ships of shallow draught could use it, and even their cargoes had to be brought through the heavy surf by local boatmen in their skiffs. The building of the great pagan city of Caesarea, with its well-made harbour, had made Joppa unimportant. It became a strong centre of Jewish feeling against pagans and against the Roman overlords.

Peter was staying with a friend of his, a tanner of Joppa named Simon. Luke's story tells how he went up on the flat roof of Simon's house, overlooking the harbour, to be alone for prayer. He fell into a trance, brought on by his great hunger. As he watched the small ships offshore, with their billowing sails, it

88

seemed that a sail came down before him, filled with animals which the Jewish Law forbade as being 'unkosher'. Jewish food-laws were strict. Only animals with split hooves, like sheep, goats and cows, could be eaten. Forbidden meat included that from pigs, dogs, rabbits (conies) as well as birds of prey and wild birds, such as the eagle, raven, hawk and heron. Jews were permitted to eat meat from domestic fowl, such as geese, hens and turkeys. The sail which Peter seemed to see contained forbidden animals. His great hunger tempted him, and three times he heard a voice bidding him to eat. He refused, and each time the voice replied: 'Do not call unclean what God has made clean.' While Peter pondered on this strange experience, messengers came seeking him. They were from Cornelius, the Roman centurion stationed at Caesarea.

Peter went back with the messengers to Caesarea. Not only did he enter the pagan city, but he also stayed at the house of

Cornelius. He preached the Christian message to Cornelius and his household, as well as his like-minded friends and relations. They believed, the power of the Spirit came upon them, and they spoke with tongues. Peter gladly baptised them. So the first Gentiles entered the Christian Church.

Jews and Gentiles in the Church

Peter had learnt a great lesson. He understood, now, the vision on the house-top. God had no favourites, no chosen people. He welcomed men of all nations into his Church, Gentiles as well as Jews. Peter, brought up in the Jewish Law, regarded Gentiles as 'different'. God made no such distinction. The proof was that he had given his Spirit to these Romans of Caesarea. It was God's doing, not his.

News of what had happened quickly reached the Church at Jerusalem. Its members, including the other apostles, were mostly Hebrews since the persecution of the Hellenists. They had been brought up strictly by the Law not to worship with Gentiles. They were appalled when they heard what Peter had done. He faced a storm when he returned to Jerusalem. He related all that had happened. It was God's doing, not his. To have refused to baptise the Gentiles would have been to defy God.

The other apostles had to agree. They were forced to accept that God welcomed Gentiles into his Church, since he gave them his Spirit. But it was not easy for them. The problem remained. Was the Christian Church simply a sect of Judaism, or was Christianity a new religion for all mankind? This was the burning problem before the Church.

To find and read in your Bible

Luke writes two books for Theophilus	Luke 1. 1–4; Acts 1. 1–5.
Luke travels with Paul	Acts 16. 10–17
Luke mentioned in Paul's letters	Colossians 4. 14; Philemon v. 24; 2 Timothy 4. 11
The first Christian Creed	Philippians 2. 11
The Day of Pentecost	Acts 2. 1–21
The Church is born	Acts 2. 37–41
Life in the Church	Acts 2. 42–47; 4. 32–35
Jewish Opposition	Acts 4. 1–22
The Church among Hebrews	Acts 5. 12–42
The Church among Hellenists	Acts 6. 1–15 and 7. 54–60
The Church among Samaritans	Acts 8. 1–17
The Church on the Coast	Acts 8. 26–40
The Church at Caesarea	Acts 10. 1–48
Jews and Gentiles in the Church	Acts 11. 1–18.

To read as a play

Read as if it was a dramatic script the story of Peter and Cornelius told in Acts 10. 1–48. You will need a reader for each part, and a narrator to read the background of the story. Put as much expression as you can into your reading parts.

To act

Act the scene, told in Acts 11. 1–18, when Peter returned to the other apostles at Jerusalem after staying with Gentiles and baptising them into the Church. Bring into your reconstruction of the meeting all the arguments that would be used on both sides.

To write out and remember

Write out the Apostles' Creed, in illuminated writing if you can. This will help you to remember it as summing up the Gospel message.

To read together

Find Isaiah 53 and read together the description of the Suffering Servant. Then discuss among the class the points that Philip would have made when he explained the meaning of the passage to the Ethiopian.

To map

Make your own map of the Jews of the Dispersion, as recorded in the story of the Day of Pentecost in Acts 2. 9–11.

To find out

Find out how the Christian Churches today observe (1) sharing, to help those in need; (2) baptism; (3) sharing of bread and wine in remembrance of the Last Supper.

To model

Make a model or plan of Jerusalem as it was in New Testament times. If you have time, make a model or plan also of the Temple. Reference books will help you with further details of the city and Temple.

To reconstruct

Reconstruct the meeting of the Jewish Council described in Acts 5. 12–42. Individual parts will be—Peter and John, speaking for the apostles; Gamaliel; the high priest as chairman. The rest of the class can be members of the Council.

To imagine

Imagine that you lived in the city of Sebaste (Samaria) rebuilt by Herod the Great. Write a letter to a friend at Jerusalem describing each of the fine buildings in your city.

To draw or paint

Design a letter-card that visitors to Caesarea might have bought in New Testament times to send home to their families. It will show a series of pictures of the chief sights of the city. You can draw or paint scenes for your letter-card.

To map

Make your own map to show how the Christian Church began to spread from Jerusalem to other cities in the Holy Land.

To explain

Give the meanings of these words which you have read about in this chapter: Gospel; evangelist; kerygma; creed; Pentecost; ghost; gift of tongues; parousia; comforter; paraclete; apocalyptic; love-feast; alms; Sanhedrin; Hebrews; Hellenists; deacon; martyr; Nazarenes; unkosher food.

To imagine

Use reference books to find out more about the Feast of Pentecost. Imagine that you came with your family from abroad as pilgrims to Jerusalem to take part in the Feast. Describe what it meant and what happened at it.

THE LIFE AND LETTERS OF PAUL

Life of Paul	Date C.E.	Letters of Paul
Birth of Paul	c.1	
Ministry of Jesus	27–29	
Stoning of Stephen	31	
Conversion of Paul	32	
Paul in the desert oasis	32–34	
Paul's 1st visit to Jerusalem	34	
Paul at Tarsus	35–44	
Paul with Barnabas at Antioch	44–45	
Paul's 2nd visit to Jerusalem	46	
First Missionary Journey	46–47	Galatians
Council of Jerusalem – Paul's 3rd visit to Jerusalem	49	
Second Missionary Journey	50–52	1 and 2 Thessalonians
Paul's 4th visit to Jerusalem	52	
Third Missionary Journey	53–56	1 and 2 Corinthians
Paul's 5th visit to Jerusalem	56	Romans
Paul a prisoner at Caesarea	56–58	
Voyage to Rome	58–59	
Paul a prisoner at Rome	59–61	Colossians; Philemon; Ephesians; Philippians
UNCERTAIN Paul released	61	
Missionary Journeys West (Spain) East (Crete, Asia Minor Macedonia, Greece)	61–64	
Paul and Peter martyred at Rome	64	1 and 2 Timothy; Titus

The Church among Gentiles

Saul of Tarsus

It is hard for us to understand how difficult it was for Jews to admit Gentiles into the Church. Only by keeping distinct from all other peoples could they be the holy people of God. Jews who had become Christians believed that Jesus of Nazareth was the Messiah. In him all the hopes and prophecies of their people were fulfilled. But was he only the Messiah of these Jews? Was the Christian Church simply a sect of Judaism? There was to be a long and bitter struggle before these questions were finally answered. The answers came through the work of the courageous missionary, Saul of Tarsus, whom we know best by the Roman form of his name—Paul.

Saul was born about the year C.E. 1 in the Roman province of Cilicia, in Asia Minor. He was justly proud of Tarsus, his home town (Acts 21. 39 and 22.3). It lay beneath the Taurus (Silver) mountains in modern Turkey. Today, 'Tersoos' is a small town of 20 000 people. In Roman times it was the chief city of Cilicia and a thriving, bustling town. It lay on the river Cydnus which linked it with the Mediterranean Sea for maritime trade. Through the town ran the ancient trade route from Mesopotamia. Thus, Tarsus was linked with both east and west and it became an important metropolis. The Romans made it the seat of government over the province of Cilicia. They gave Roman citizenship to its people, as well as self-government and freedom from taxation. Tarsus had a fine university, for its people were eager philosophers—keener, said one writer, than the men of Athens or Alexandria. From Tarsus came a great Stoic philosopher named Athenodorus, who was a tutor of Augustus Caesar. When he retired to Tarsus he helped to build the fame of its univeristy. No wonder a man from Tarsus was proud of his city.

In Tarsus the culture of Greece and oriental customs were both common, as east and west met there. Saul as a result was familiar with both. He knew something of Greek philosophy, poetry, sculpture, architecture and religion. But he was accustomed, on the other hand, to the oriental custom of women covering their heads, and he advised that women should do this in the Church (1 Corinthians 11. 3–6). The main industries of Tarsus came from its fine timber and from the famous Cilician goats. Still today there is a street of weavers in Tersoos, weaving goat's-hair from the herds in the Taurus Mountains. From their hair came a tough cloth, famous for its strength, called 'cilicium'. Hence the French word 'cilice' meaning 'cloak'. Tents and sails, as well as cloaks, were made from it. Saul's father would have been in this cloth trade. Every Jewish boy was taught a trade, no matter what career he was to follow. Usually he learnt the trade of his father. Saul was destined to be a scholar of the Jewish Law. But he had to learn a trade, like every other Jewish boy, so that he could always support himself, whatever happened. That is why we read that, when necessary, he supported himself by tent-making (Acts 18. 3 and 20. 34), and could boast that he had never been a burden to anyone.

Saul the man

Jesus had been a country boy, and the stories and illustrations that he used in his teaching naturally came from country life. Saul was a town boy, and he naturally drew pictures from city life. He writes of butchers selling meat, buildings with their workmen, slaves being branded, tax-collectors, soldiers, athletes, boxers.

That was the background of his boyhood in Tarsus. But he also had a strict upbringing from his Jewish parents who wanted him to become a rabbi, a teacher of the Law. He had a good education and after going to the local synagogue school, and then perhaps to a private tutor, he went to Jerusalem to study under the famous rabbi Gamaliel. Jerusalem was the 'university' of the Jews, so that Saul had the finest education possible for any Jewish boy. He was a devout Pharisee, dedicated to the sacred Law of his people (Acts 26. 5; Philippians 3. 5).

As a Hellenist, a Jew from abroad, Saul spoke Greek as his everyday language. But he had also learnt Aramaic, the language of the Jews in Judaea, and he must have known at least some Latin, the language of the Romans. In his speeches and letters he quotes from almost every book of the Old Testament, showing how good a scholar he was. His quotations come, as we should expect, from the Septuagint, the Greek version of the Jewish Scriptures.

Inside the Gymnasium

The victor crowned in the Stadium

PAGAN CITIES

GERASA—A RECONSTRUCTION

Theatre

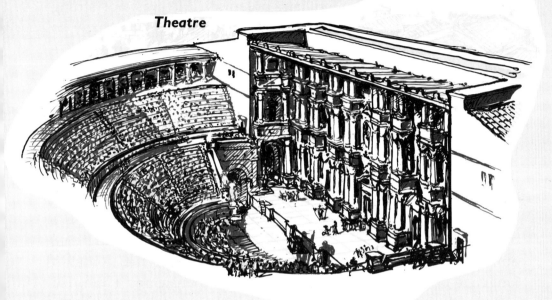

Domestic Life

A house where Cornelius the centurion might have lived

Saul was a man of great energy and a born leader. He was a powerful speaker and a brilliant organiser. He was not strong physically, though he was wiry and determined and ready to endure anything. He suffered from a disease which may have been epilepsy or malaria, for it often recurred. He seems to have been short in body, and only distinguished by his fiery speech. One writer of a century later said that he was bald and hook-nosed, but we cannot rely on this. One certain fact is that Saul suffered terrible hardships all through his life (2 Corinthians 11. 22–30), and these must have left their mark upon his body. Yet nothing could ever daunt this courageous Christian warrior.

In all these ways Saul was wonderfully equipped to be a missionary. He was a Roman citizen, protected by imperial authority wherever he went. He spoke Greek, the common language of the Roman world, as well as Aramaic and Latin. He was familiar with Greek culture and with oriental customs. He had a first-class Jewish education. He may have had some private means, but he could always support himself by his trade. Added to all these were his outstanding abilities as an orator, and organ-iser, a leader. No one could have been better equipped to travel the Roman world.

Saul becomes Paul

Although Saul was in Jerusalem during the ministry of Jesus, he never seems to have met him. If he had, he would have proudly proclaimed it again and again. But he had an experience of Jesus that was to change his whole life.

Saul was immersed in his study of the Law at Jerusalem. He

must have seemed very narrow in his outlook to Gamaliel. The great rabbi was tolerant and liberal in his interpretation of the Law. He had advised the Council of the Jewish leaders not to persecute Christians. Saul was eager to attack them. It seems that he was a member of the Council himself, for he speaks later of having given his vote against the Nazarenes, as the followers of Jesus of Nazareth were called. It was Saul who stood by at the stoning of Stephen, the first Christian martyr. It was at his feet that the members of the Council laid their cloaks so as to free their arms for the stoning. The lynching of Stephen was only the beginning of persecution. It was directed against the Hellenists, the more liberal Jews from abroad, who had begun to teach that the Law and the Temple were no longer necessary. Such followers of Jesus were no longer Jews. They were heretics and traitors to their people. They were known as followers of the 'Way' (Acts 19. 23)—the 'Way of Salvation' (Acts 16. 17) through faith in Jesus.

Saul took an active part in this persecution. But he was not content with tracking down Christians in Jerusalem and having them dragged off to prison. He asked for authority from the high priest to go after Christians who had fled to Damascus, and to bring them back for trial at Jerusalem. The zealous persecutor set off eagerly on the road to Damascus, the armed guards scarcely able to keep up with him.

It was about 225 km from Jerusalem to Damascus along the sandy road, baked by the sun. It would take about six days. Saul was almost in sight of Damascus when he had the experience that was to change his life. He often referred to it in his writings, and we are given three accounts of it in Luke's writings (Acts 9. 1–30; 22. 3–16; 26. 9–18). The light that overwhelmed him may have been lightning or the blazing sun. But the experience was within himself. He heard the voice of Jesus calling him. The doubts in his unconscious mind had made him more and more fierce in his persecution of Christianity. They must have started when he watched Stephen die, fearless and uncomplaining, inspired by his faith and assurance of the presence of Jesus. He must have seen many other Christians, since that day, ready to suffer for their faith. Saul could never admit their faith and courage and the truth they believed. But doubts had gone on growing, deep in his mind, and now they burst into his consciousness. So great was their force that Saul temporarily lost his sight. The fierce persecutor was led, helpless and shocked, into the city of Damascus. He was found lodging at the house of a certain Judas in Straight Street.

Damascus had always been a key city. It was the meeting-place of three great caravan routes—the highways that led south-west to Egypt, south to the peninsula of Arabia, and east to Mesopotamia. It owed its existence to the waters of the river Abana—today the Barada river—whose streams made a well-watered plain. All through Old Testament times Damascus had been an important city. The building of Antioch made Damascus less important, but it was completely rebuilt in the Greek period. A Greek named Hippodamas, of the fifth century B.C.E., had become famous as a town-planner. Damascus was rebuilt according to his plans which, for a new city, would mean perfectly straight streets and roads crossing each other at exact right-angles. For an old city such as Damascus the plan had to be adapted. Damascus was rebuilt as a rectangle, with the river along one of its sides. The longest thoroughfare was called Straight Street and it was lined with colonnades and shops, as in every Greek city. Today it is called Suk-el-Tawileh, 'The Long Street', and it is still the chief road through the Old City and still has shops on each side as in Roman times. The rebuilt city had a temple dedicated to its ancient god, Hadad, a great temple in honour of Jupiter-Zeus, and a royal palace and citadel.

Damascus had long been a centre of the Jewish Dispersion. It had a large colony of Jewish merchants and tradesmen—perhaps working in the cloth trade, from which we get our word 'damask'. In New Testament times, the rebuilt city of Damascus was one of the towns which were linked together in the league of Greek cities known as the Decapolis.

STRAIGHT STREET IN DAMASCUS

Reconstruction of the time of St. Paul

Today

For three days Saul lay sightless in his lodging, without food or drink. His overwhelming experience had destroyed all that he had lived by. He was helpless and bewildered. Then there came to him a certain brave Christian named Ananias, guided to visit the Jew who had come to persecute him and his brethren. By the laying on of his hands he brought healing and peace to this man, who was to take the new name of Paul, and baptised him into the Christian Church.

Paul preaches the Good News

At once Paul began preaching in the synagogues of Damascus. It seems that he met with little success, and we can understand why. It was not easy for Christian Jews to forget that Paul had come to persecute them. Strict Jews must have been just as astonished, and then increasingly angry. Moreover, he was ill-prepared for proclaiming Christianity. He had not been instructed in the faith. He had not thought out what it meant for either Jews or Gentiles. Wisely he decided to go away to think out his new faith. He spent some three years at an oasis in the desert, probably on the borders of Syria near to Damascus (Galatians 1. 17).

On his return to Damascus, Paul preached with great success in the synagogues. But success brought him enemies. Jewish opponents denounced him to the Governor of Damascus, an official of the king of the Nabataean people, Aretas IV. His kingdom stretched all around the south and east of the Holy Land, and he had now extended his territory as far as Damascus. (See

THE NABATAEANS

The Nabataeans were a tribe of Arab nomads. They drove out the Edomites and made Petra their capital. They became rich merchants by controlling the caravan routes between the Red Sea, Arabia and the Persian Gulf. Their greatest king Aretas IV (9 B.C.E. to C.E. 40) was father-in-law of Herod Antipas, ruler of Galilee in the time of Jesus. Aretas was in control of Damascus when Paul was there.

Caravans came to Petra from as far away as Africa, India and even China. Goods were sent on to Gaza and then shipped to Greece and Rome. Thus the Nabataeans were a powerful and wealthy people. Archaeologists have found much evidence of their fine culture, too. Their capital, Petra, can still only be approached on foot or by donkey. It is a beautiful 'rose-red city, half as old as time'.

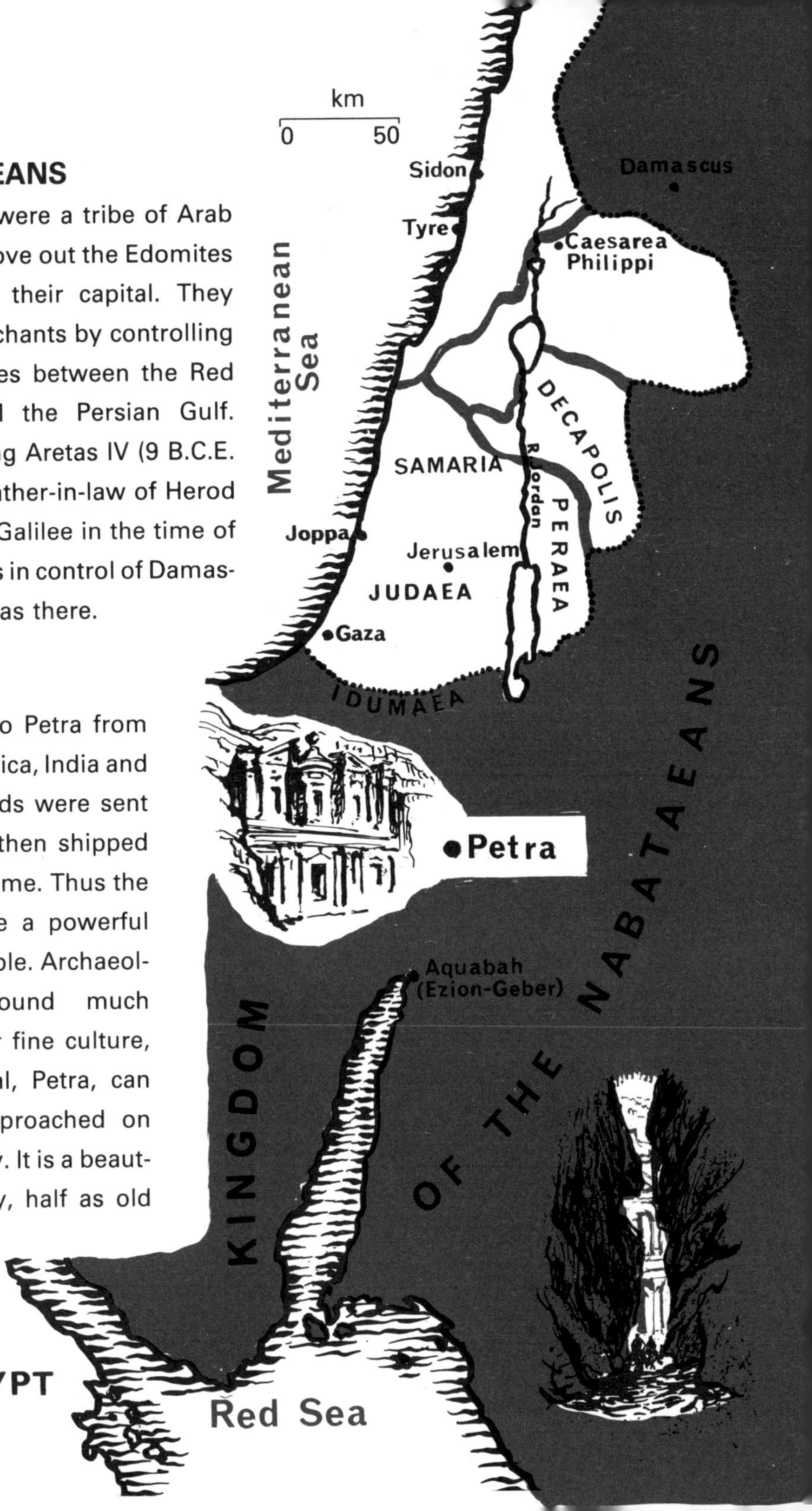

km
0   50

Sidon
Damascus
Tyre
Caesarea Philippi
Mediterranean Sea
DECAPOLIS
SAMARIA
R. Jordan
PERAEA
Joppa
Jerusalem
JUDAEA
Gaza
IDUMAEA

●Petra

Aquabah
(Ezion-Geber)

KINGDOM   OF   THE   NABATAEANS

EGYPT
Red Sea

map on page 105.) Orders were given for the arrest of Paul, now in hiding, and the city gates were watched to prevent his escape (2 Corinthians 11. 32–33). Paul's Christian friends lowered him out of the window of a house on the city wall in a large basket. It was the first of many dangerous adventures.

Paul at Jerusalem

Paul made his way back to Jerusalem and there he was befriended by a Christian Jew name Barnabas. A Levite by birth, Barnabas had the privilege of taking part in the worship of the Temple. He would thus be approved by strict Jews. But he was also a Hellenist, one of the Greek-speaking Jews from abroad, and he was therefore much more liberal in his interpretation of the Law. He was the uncle of Mark, and he would naturally stay at Mark's home when he was in Jerusalem. But this was the headquarters of the Christians in Jerusalem, and we can understand therefore how Barnabas became a Christian. He had soon shown his devotion by selling a plot of land he owned near Jerusalem and giving the money to the Church.

Barnabas came from the island of Cyprus. It lay just off the mainland of Asia Minor, 80 km from Tarsus, the home of Paul. They would have much in common with each other. Barnabas introduced Paul to the church at Jerusalem, vouching for him as a genuine believer. The Christian group at Jerusalem knew Paul as their former persecutor, and they were naturally afraid of him. It was only through the friendship of Barnabas that he became accepted among them. Paul learnt much from Peter and also from James, the brother of Jesus, now a leader in the Church (Galatians

TAURUS MTS.

Cilician Gates

● Tarsus

ANTIOCH

Seleucia ●

R. Orontes

Mediterranean Sea

Sidon ●

● Damascus

Tyre ●

CAESAREA ●

Joppa ●

JERUSALEM ●

THE EARLY JOURNEYS
OF PAUL

km

0   50   100

1. 18–19). In his letters Paul quoted what he had learnt from them—the story of the Last Supper (1 Corinthians 11. 23–25), and the appearances of Jesus after his crucifixion (1 Corinthians 15. 3–8), as well as sayings of Jesus (e.g. Acts 20, 35).

Paul quickly made enemies among Jews by his preaching of Jesus as the Messiah. Again he was forced to flee. Members of the Church realised that his life would be in danger if he stayed in Jerusalem. They accompanied him to the port of Caesarea, 102 km away. There Paul took ship to Tarsus.

The Church at Antioch

Paul spent the next ten years in Cilicia (Galatians 1. 21), mostly, no doubt, in his home town of Tarsus. There he would have plenty of opportunity to proclaim his faith both among Jews in their synagogues and among Gentiles in the streets and in the university. It is probable that he devoted himself mainly to Jews, and their opposition may well account for some of the many sufferings which he lists in one of his letters (2 Corinthians 11. 22–30). His name would have become known to the Christians in the lively church at Antioch, 130 km from Tarsus.

Antioch, capital of the Roman province of Syria, was the third largest city in the whole of the Roman empire. It was known as 'Antioch the Great' and 'Queen of the East'. It lay on the river Orontes, some 480 km to the north of Jerusalem, and about 30 km from its seaport named Seleucia. To it came ships from the western world and caravans from all over the east, making Antioch a great cosmopolitan city. A long street ran right through Antioch, as was common in Greek cities, and it had the usual colonnades and shops on either side. In its remains were found street lamps, dating from about 400 years later.

The population of the city was about 200 000, and they enjoyed all the customary Greek buildings—theatres, stadia, baths, and amphitheatres. Antioch could also boast of itself as a centre of learning, for it possessed a famous library and students came from far and near to study philosophy, medicine and rhetoric.

But Antioch was famed for pleasure rather than for learning. Near to the city was Daphne, the famous centre of the worship of Apollo. The shrine of the god was surrounded by a vast pleasure-park, 16 km round, with groves and gardens where all kinds of pleasures and vices could be enjoyed. The patron goddess of Antioch was 'Fortune' ('Tyche'), but many others were worship-ped. In the great city were gods and creeds and customs from both east and west. The people of Antioch were famous for their love of pleasure, their quick tongues and their ready wits. It was here, for example, that the followers of Jesus were nicknamed 'Christians'. Antioch was a pagan and worldly city where every vice flourished. Yet it was to be the first great missionary centre of Christianity from which the Gospel was to spread up into Asia Minor and across to Europe.

The stoning of Stephen had been followed by persecution of Hellenist Jews, and many fled from Jerusalem. Some, as we have seen, went to Damascus. Others travelled even further, some to Cyprus and others to Antioch in Syria. In Antioch they found a large Jewish colony, well-established in the commercial life of the city. Jews also enjoyed all the rights of citizens of this free city. The Christian preachers naturally proclaimed their faith first in the synagogues. They received a warm welcome from the God-fearers

ANTIOCH IN SYRIA

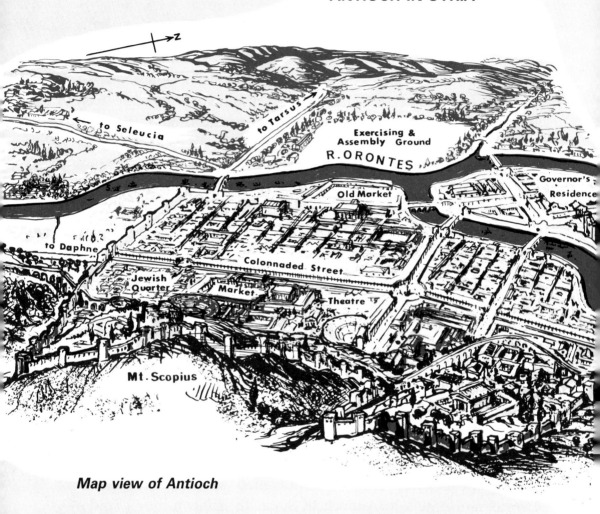

Map view of Antioch

Antioch, on the river Orontes, about 30 km from the Mediterranean Sea, was the third largest city in the Roman Empire. Its population was about 200 000. The city was destroyed in the sixth century C.E. Today it is a small Turkish town, Antakiyeh, of about 35 000.

The Goddess Tyche, with the River Orontes swimming before her

Antioch today, seen across the Orontes.

odrome

to Beroea (Aleppo)

Pleasure grounds at Daphne

and many were baptised. So was born the first Gentile church (Acts 11. 19–21).

Now, for the first time, Gentiles and Jews met together in the brotherhood of the Church. They sat side by side at table in the meal of fellowship. This was revolutionary. When the news reached the Jewish Christians at Jerusalem they would receive it with astonishment, if not with horror. Already Peter had mixed with a household of Gentiles and baptised them. But that could be regarded as exceptional. It was quite different when a new church grew up in which Jews were outnumbered by Gentiles, and in which Jews and Gentiles met regularly together.

Barnabas was sent from Jerusalem to look into the happenings at Antioch. As a man of Cyprus he was a good choice, for he knew the area and its people well and the church at Antioch had been founded by fellow-countrymen of his. He was delighted by what he found at Antioch. The young church there was full of life and growing fast. The Spirit of God was clearly at work in it. Here was a wonderful opportunity for spreading the Gospel, not only in Antioch but beyond the city. To Barnabas, a Hellenist, it mattered little that the church of Antioch was Gentile rather than Jewish. But he saw that it needed leaders and he had not forgotten Paul, a name that must already have been known to the Christians of Antioch. Barnabas went to Tarsus, 130 km away, to fetch Paul.

They took ship back to Seleucia, the port of Antioch, and so began their work together as leaders of the first Gentile church. It was C.E. 45. For a year they worked side by side at Antioch.

Paul's first missionary journey, C.E. 46–47

Though the church at Antioch was made up mostly of Gentiles, it had a strong sense of loyalty to the mother church at Jerusalem. When news came of famine in Judaea it was quickly decided to send help. A collection was made, and Barnabas and Paul were chosen to take it to Jerusalem for the relief of the needy brethren there.

But Gentile Christians had the whole world to minister to, and, as their church grew in numbers and enthusiasm, there came a natural desire to spread the Gospel message. We have already seen two ways by which the Gospel was spread. One was persecution, which always had the opposite effect to what was intended. Men who fled from persecution took their faith wherever they went, and so scattered more seed. A second way in which the message carried further afield was through ordinary people. They

HOW THE GOSPEL WAS SPREAD

'Ye shall be witnesses unto me both in Jerusalem, and in all Judaea, and in Samaria, and unto the uttermost part of the earth' (Acts 1.8).

The Church grew through:

1. Persecution (Acts 8.4)
2. Ordinary people (Acts 18.2)
3. Missionary work (Acts 13.2)

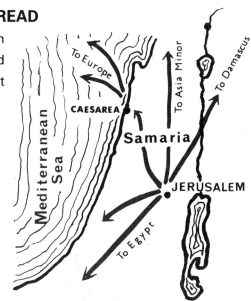

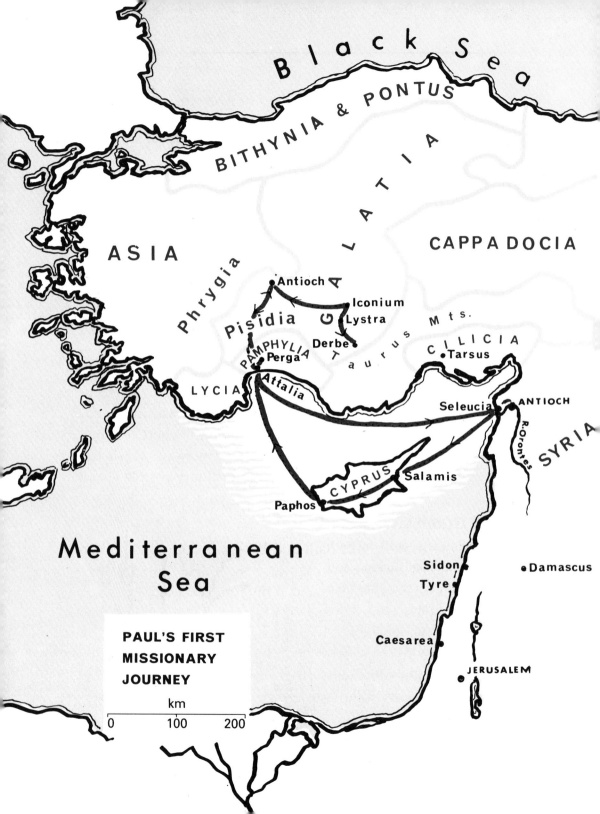

Black Sea

BITHYNIA & PONTUS

ASIA

Phrygia

Pisidia

Antioch

Iconium
Lystra

Derbe

Perga

PAMPHYLIA

Attalia

LYCIA

G A L A T I A

CAPPADOCIA

T a u r u s   M t s.

CILICIA

Tarsus

Seleucia

ANTIOCH

R. Orontes

SYRIA

CYPRUS

Salamis

Paphos

Mediterranean
Sea

Sidon

Tyre

Damascus

Caesarea

JERUSALEM

PAUL'S FIRST
MISSIONARY
JOURNEY

km

0   100   200

too took their faith with them when their work called them to a new town or a new country. Now we find the Gospel being spread in a third way—by deliberate missionary work. Barnabas and Paul were the obvious leaders of this first missionary effort of the church at Antioch. It had other leaders, 'prophets' and 'teachers', who could carry on during their absence. Two of those named were men from Africa.

Paul and Barnabas set out from Antioch with the blessing of the whole church there. They took with them the young nephew of Barnabas, Mark. The first stage of the journey took them 27 km to Seleucia, the port of Antioch. 'Seleucia Pieria', 'Seleucia the Stony', it was called, even though it had been built on the only piece of flat land along that part of the coast. Seleucia had been fortified by the Romans and made a free city. It was an important harbour for commerce in the time of Paul, linking Antioch with the western world.

The Church in Cyprus

Barnabas naturally longed to preach the Gospel in his own island of Cyprus, and the party sailed across to it. There were already a few Christians on the island, Hellenists who had fled from the persecution in Jerusalem. But Paul and Barnabas had great ambitions to establish new churches. That is why we find them going to the two main towns on the island. This was good strategy, for from a large town the Gospel could spread out into the countryside.

Cyprus was 100 km from Seleucia. The island is shaped like a fist, it has often been said, with the forefinger pointing to Syrian Antioch. From its two mountain ranges came valuable timber and the precious copper from which Cyprus got its name. The island had already been part of the Roman empire for a century. One of its Governors had been Cicero, the famous Roman orator.

The missionaries landed at Salamis, the nearest port to Antioch on the island. It was the largest port, too, founded centuries before by Phoenician traders, and the island's main trading centre for the copper, olive oil and fruits which it exported. Salamis boasted a famous temple dedicated to Jupiter-Zeus, the father of the gods. But there was a colony of Jewish traders in the port, as in all great commercial centres. Paul and Barnabas naturally made their way to the Jewish quarter and spoke in the synagogues. This was a well-planned move, for the synagogue congregation of Jews and God-fearers was a ready-made audience for the Gospel message.

Leaving Salamis, the missionaries made their way through the island to its capital, the city of Paphos, at the other end. Here was the seat of the Roman Proconsul, Sergius Paulus, who ruled over Cyprus. A stone inscription, found in modern times, bears his name. It is dated about C.E. 55 but it refers to the time years before when Paul had visited the island. It shows us, too, that Luke was correct both in the title and name of the Roman official on the island.

Paphos also had been founded by Phoenician traders, long before. Besides being a trading city and the seat of government, it was a centre of pagan religion. Pagans believed that Aphrodite—the Roman Venus, goddess of love and of the fruitfulness of nature—rose here from the sea. This belief was the origin of her Greek name ('aphros'—'sea foam'). Pilgrims came from near and far to the temple of Aphrodite at Paphos, which was almost as famous as the temple of Diana at Ephesus.

Paphos

Aphrodite – Venus
Paphos was the great centre of
the worship of this goddess.

PAGAN GODDESSES WORSHIPPED IN THE CITITES VISITED BY PAUL

Artemis – Diana
Perga was a centre of the
worship of the ancient nature-
goddess, 'Queen of Perga'.
Artemis was worshipped by
nomadic hunters of earlier tribes
who thought that the wild
animals belonged to her.

Ruins at Perga

But the crude rites and superstitious nonsense of the cult of the goddess meant nothing to Sergius Paulus, the thoughtful and intelligent Proconsul. He sent for Paul and Barnabas, asking to hear their new teaching. Despite the opposition and tricks of a sorcerer, it seems that Paul had a great effect upon the Proconsul. If he did become a Christian, as Luke seems to imply, it was a great victory for Paul. It is interesting that Luke begins, at this point in his history, to use the Roman name 'Paul' rather than 'Saul'. It is now, too, that Paul takes the place of Barnabas as leader of the missionary party. This first meeting with an important Roman official certainly illustrates Luke's main argument—that, while Jews could not accept the Gospel message, Gentiles welcomed it and, in particular, Roman officials were friendly to the Christian preachers.

The Church in Asia Minor

Paul and his companions sailed from Paphos to the mainland of Asia Minor. The voyage of 275 km brought them to the Roman province of Pamphylia. They went up-river to Perga, a pagan town in an area where fever was prevalent. Perga had long been a centre of the worship of the ancient nature-goddess named Artemis. The goddess had become identified with Diana, the Greek and Roman goddess of the hunt, and the maiden sister of Apollo the sun-god. Artemis was, in fact, known as 'Queen of Perga'.

The missionaries did not stop at Perga. Paul was anxious to press inland over the mountains. It may be, too, that, suffering from malaria, his only hope was to get away from the marshy, fever-ridden plain up into the healthy mountain region. The

journey ahead was long, difficult and dangerous. This may be the reason why young Mark left the party at Perga and went back to his home in Jerusalem. He may have been afraid of the many dangers ahead, especially from bandits and wild beasts. He may have been jealous of Paul who was overshadowing his uncle Barnabas more and more. He may have been simply homesick. Whatever the reason, he deserted the missionaries. Paul did not forget. He refused to take Mark on his next journey and, as a result, Paul and Barnabas went their separate ways. But Mark was to prove himself in time, and to become a pillar of strength to Paul. When Paul was a prisoner at Rome, years later, he refers to Mark in his letters as his faithful companion (Colossians 4. 10; Philemon v. 24; 2 Timothy 4. 11). And, of course, it is to Mark that we owe the very first Christian gospel.

1. Antioch in Pisidia

Paul and Barnabas left the hot, flat plain, with its swamps and malaria, and journeyed 160 km inland over the mountains to the north. Paul was welcomed with great kindness by the mountain people of Galatia. He was doubly grateful for it because he was ill at the time, and he remembered their kindness (Galatians 4. 13–15).

Once they were on the healthier highlands, Paul made for the largest town in the district. He always followed this plan. A populous city would be a fine centre for spreading the Gospel. It would also have a colony of Jewish traders whose synagogues would give him an audience of Hellenist Jews and God-fearers. So he made for Antioch, in Pisidia. We must be careful to distinguish it from the Antioch in Syria from which the missionaries had started on their journey.

Pisidian Antioch was the centre of Roman rule in the province of Galatia. It controlled the main trade route between the large city of Ephesus and Cilicia. The Romans had made it a free city, so that the citizens governed themselves. Their Assembly, or city council, was called the 'ekklesia', from a Greek word meaning 'the calling out'—that is, the assembly of citizens called out by the town crier. Christians took over this word to describe their own assembly of believers. From it come our words 'ecclesiastic' and 'ecclesiastical'.

This Antioch was a Roman colony, and archaeologists have found the remains of its fine arched aqueduct which brought water to the city, and of triumphal arches covered with reliefs. They recorded the victories of Augustus Caesar on land and sea, telling

ROMAN AQUEDUCT AT ANTIOCH IN PISIDIA
(*a reconstruction*)

Section

of the 'Deeds Accomplished by the Divine Augustus'. Antioch had a patron god called 'Men', worshipped under the symbol of a bull's head, but there were many pagan gods worshipped in Asia Minor. Most popular of all was Cybele, mother goddess of nature and of fertility, whom the Greeks identified with their Artemis, their early nature goddess. Antioch boasted a temple of Cybele where the popular pagan rites were held.

COIN FROM ANTIOCH

STATUE OF THE GODDESS CYBELE

The representation of Artemis as Earth Mother at Ephesus

Paul's first address in the synagogue at Antioch won some Jews, but his greatest success was with the God-fearers. They asked if they might hear him again. A great crowd gathered on the following sabbath, causing jealousy among the Jews. They interrupted Paul's address, arguing with him, contradicting him, and shouting him down. It was now that Paul bluntly proclaimed that, since the Jews rejected the Gospel, he would turn to the Gentiles. The God-fearers were delighted at this, and many were won to the Church; so too, were certain of the Jews. But strict Jews stirred up opposition to Paul and Barnabas. They used devout and influential women to make accusations to the magistrates. They had the missionaries expelled from the city on charges of causing public disorder.

2. Iconium

Paul was undaunted. The seed had been sown at Antioch, and he left behind him the beginnings of a church. He went on to the town of Iconium, 100 km to the east—today the Turkish town of Konya. It lay on the main trade route between Ephesus and Syria, and it was an important centre of trade. Under the Greeks and Romans it became the chief city of Phrygia. It lay in a well-watered oasis, famous for its orchards which produced apricots and plums.

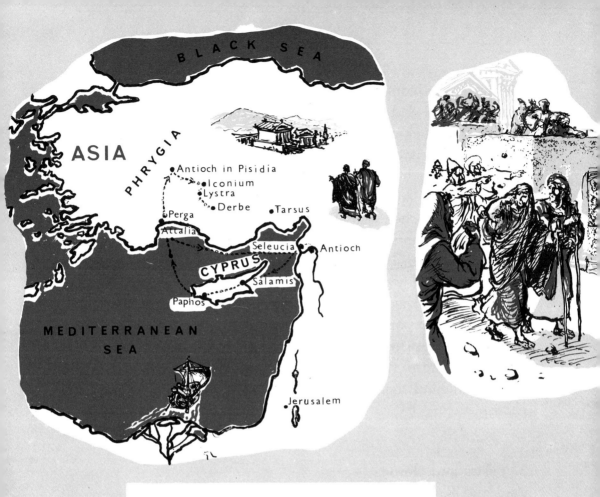

**PAUL'S FIRST MISSIONARY
JOURNEY**

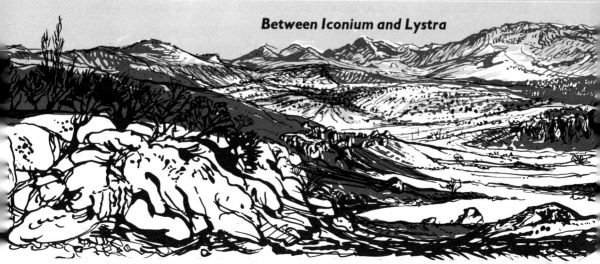

Between Iconium and Lystra

The people of Iconium also grew flax, and made rugs and textiles from the wool and hair of their mountain sheep and goats. This, too, was a Greek city.

Paul and Barnabas made a long stay at Iconium. They had much success among both Jews and Greeks. But inevitably, too, they made enemies among Jews who held strictly to the traditional faith. Paul preached that all the hopes and prophecies of the Jews had already been fulfilled in Jesus of Nazareth. He was the long-awaited Messiah. But this was blasphemy to Jews who could not accept Jesus. They were displeased at the success of the Christian preachers who had won both Jews and Gentiles to their faith. They stirred up popular feeling and a plot was made to stone Paul and Barnabas. The missionaries heard of the intrigues against them, and had to flee the city to save themselves. But once again they left behind them a group of believers as the beginnings of a church.

3. Lystra and Derbe

Paul and Barnabas went on to Lystra, a smaller town, some 40 km south-west of Iconium. The site of the town was made certain when, in 1885, a stone altar was found, still standing upright as it had stood in the time of Paul. On it was a Latin inscription stating that this was the site of a Roman colony. It was dedicated to Augustus Caesar, who had founded the colony in 6 B.C.E. The name of the colony, given on the inscription, was 'Lustra'.

One happening at Lystra shows clearly the simple and superstitious religion of the pagan people of Asia Minor. Paul had healed a crippled man, and at once the townsfolk hailed Paul and

A slave leading a bull adorned with garlands, ready for sacrifice. From a relief discovered at Rome.

Jupiter (Zeus),
father of the gods

Mercury (Hermes),
messenger of the
gods

Barnabas as gods come down to earth in human form. Barnabas was the older man, the taller, more robust and imposing of the two visitors. He must be Zeus, father of all the gods of Olympus, known to the Romans as Jupiter. Paul was smaller, less imposing, but a man of energy and of fiery speech. He must be Hermes, the herald and messenger of the gods, known to the Romans as Mercury. The Greek forms of these names are given in the original manuscripts of the New Testament. But the old English translation of the Bible gave their Latin form, for these would be more familiar to English people.

At once the people of Lystra made ready to sacrifice to these gods, to honour them and celebrate their wonderful visitation. The gods were worshipped by pagans with animal sacrifices. The priest of the temple of Zeus fetched oxen and placed garlands around their necks, as the custom was, ready for the sacrifice. Paul and Barnabas were horrified, but it was almost impossible for them to restrain the excited, joyous crowds of pagans. It was difficult, too, to make themselves understood to people who spoke their own local dialect. The missionaries tore their clothes in dramatic protest. They pushed into the crowds, crying out to them to stop, shouting that they were men and not gods. When at last they got a hearing, Paul appealed to the simple pagans to give up their empty worship and to turn to the living God, Lord and Creator of all things. It was he who gave the rain and the sun and growth to the crops—not imaginary gods and goddesses.

The missionaries had little time to win over the people of Lystra. Jewish opponents arrived from both Antioch and Iconium. They stirred up a mob and attacked Paul. He was stoned, dragged out of the city, and left for dead. But, cared for by believers, he recovered consciousness. Again he had to move on. But again he left new Christian believers as a result of his visit.

Paul and Barnabas went on a further 30 km to the town of

Derbe. Both Lystra and Derbe were small places and neither of them seems to have had a Jewish colony. There was therefore no synagogue at which to make a start. But there is no record of opposition at Derbe, and the preaching of the Gospel seems to have met with success.

Lystra and Derbe are important in the story of the early Church for another reason, besides the founding of their churches. Paul was beginning to gather disciples around him who could help in his ministry, and carry on his work after him. It was from these two small towns that Timothy and Gaius came. Both were to travel with Paul and to become leaders in the Church.

The return to Syrian Antioch

Derbe was the limit of this first missionary journey. Now came the return to Antioch. It would have been easy to have gone from Derbe through the mountain pass to Tarsus, and then back by ship to Syrian Antioch. But Paul, the brilliant organiser, was determined to go back the way he had come, visiting and strengthening the churches he had founded. So he and Barnabas retraced their journey, going back to Lystra, Iconium and Pisidian Antioch. There was no need, this time, to go to the Jewish synagogues and to create new riots. These were private visits, for Paul could now go directly to the group of believers he had left behind him, both Jews and Gentiles, meeting in a private house. He had three things to do. The first was to strengthen each church in the faith and to encourage its members to be ready to stand up and to suffer for their faith, if need be, as he had done. The second was to encourage each group of Christians to be a missionary church. Each was

PAUL'S MISSIONARY STRAGEGY

1. He set up churches in key towns.
From them the Good News would be carried to small towns and villages in the country round about.

2. He appointed elders for each church.
These ministers looked after the life and worship of the churches as 'overseers'. They cared for their members as 'shepherds'.

3. He re-visited his churches.
Paul carefully planned his missionary journeys so that he went back again to churches he had founded, and strengthened them in their Christian faith and life.

4. He kept in touch with his churches by letters.
During his absences, Paul kept in touch with his churches by letters. They were sent by the regular Roman post, or carried by messengers. They dealt with problems which had arisen. There are 21 Letters or 'Epistles' among the 27 books of the New Testament. Of these, 9 were definitely written by Paul, and four others may also have come originally from him.

in a key town. Each could be the base for missionary work in the surrounding country.

But each church needed leaders, above all. Paul copied the organisation of the Jewish synagogue. For each church he chose and appointed good men as 'elders'. Their work is shown by the various words used to describe them. An elder controlled the affairs of his churches as 'overseer'. The Greek word for this was 'episcopos', from which we get our word 'episcopal' to describe a bishop. For our word 'bishop' comes from the Old English 'biscop' which means 'overseer'. An elder also led the worship of his church and cared for its members as a 'shepherd'. Christian ministers were called 'pastors' (Latin 'pastor'—'shepherd') because they cared for their people as a shepherd cares for his sheep.

On his return journey, therefore, we find Paul appointing elders for the churches of Lystra, Iconium and Pisidian Antioch. These private visits were uneventful. Only at Antioch had Paul and Barnabas been officially expelled. But by now the new annual magistrates had been appointed, so that the order made against them was no longer in force. Paul was able to concentrate simply on the ordering of his churches. Nor was this the end of his contact with them. He was to visit them again, whenever he could. During his absence, he kept in touch with them by letters. One of Paul's letters in the New Testament was addressed to 'The Galatians'. It seems to have been a joint letter, sent to his churches at Antioch, Iconium, Lystra and Derbe.

Paul did not forget the persecution he had suffered on this first missionary journey. He quoted it to his disciple, Timothy, as an example of suffering for the sake of the Gospel (2 Timothy 3. 10–11). Throughout the rest of his life Paul was consistently opposed by Jews. They saw Paul's message as blasphemous and they saw Paul as a perverter of Jewish teaching.

Paul and Barnabas made their way back to the coast, stopping at Lystra, Iconium and Antioch. They passed through Perga again, taking the opportunity to preach there. They took ship from Attalia, 26 km away, and sailed back direct to Syrian Antioch. They had been travelling for nearly two years. They had journeyed 2,250 km by land and sea. They had planted churches in both Cyprus and Asia Minor.

They were given a great welcome back by the Christians of Syrian Antioch. The whole church gathered to hear the story of all that they had done. But they felt it was the story of what God had done. One thing seemed clear to them. God welcomed Gentiles into his Church. Jews had generally not accepted the belief in Jesus of Nazareth as their Messiah. Some had believed, others had been bitterly hostile. But it was Gentiles above all who welcomed the Christian message and were baptised into the Church. God had given them faith and the power of his Spirit.

To find and read in your Bible

Saul of Tarsus	Acts 21. 39 and 22.3
Saul's trade as a tent-maker	Acts 18. 3 and 20. 34

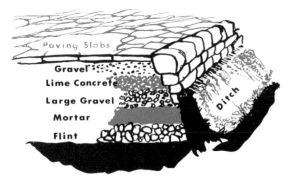

Paving Slabs
Gravel
Lime Concrete
Large Gravel
Mortar
Flint
Ditch

ROMAN ROADS

Paul was greatly helped on his journeys by the wonderful Roman system of roads. Many still remain today. Roman milestones can also be seen. They were set up at every 1000 paces along the dead-straight Roman roads.

Saul a strict Pharisee	Acts 26. 5
Saul becomes Paul the Christian	Acts 9. 1–30
Paul at an oasis in the desert	Galatians 1. 17
Paul returns to Tarsus	Acts 9. 20–30
The Gentile church at Antioch in Syria	Acts 11. 19–26
Paul's first missionary journey-Cyprus	Acts 13. 4–12
Antioch in Pisidia	Acts 13. 13–50
Iconium	Acts 13. 51–14. 5
Lystra	Acts 14. 6–20
Derbe	Acts 14. 20–21
The return to Syrian Antioch	Acts 14. 21–28

Milestone

To map
Make your own map of the eastern end of the Mediterranean Sea.
Show on it the journeys of Paul, related in this chapter, and the
towns which have been mentioned.

To play a role
Imagine you were one of the soldiers sent with Paul to Damascus
to bring Christian prisoners back to Jerusalem. Describe what
happened to Paul on the road to Damascus, and what became of
him after you had led him into the city.

To design
Design a letter-card for the city of Antioch in Syria. It will consist

*Road of paving blocks
on rocky ground
running between
Antioch and Aleppo.*

of pictures of all the main sights in and around the city—especially the main street. This letter-card would be on sale for visitors to the city. You can, if you wish, write a letter on the back of your letter-card, describing the town, to send to your cousin in Rome.

To research
Use reference books to find out more about the Roman gods and goddesses mentioned in this chapter. Write an account of them, with your own drawings. Say why you think men like Sergius Paulus, the Roman Governor of Cyprus, could not believe in these gods.

To report
Imagine you were a newspaper reporter at Lystra. Write a report for your readers of what happened when Paul and Barnabas visited the town, including what Paul said to the crowd.

To write out
Here are some famous passages from the Letters of Paul. Writing them out will help you to remember them:

The love of God in Jesus	Romans 8. 38–39
One in Christ	Galatians 3. 26–28
The man of God	1 Timothy 6. 11–12
A prayer	Philippians 4. 7

To make a strip cartoon
Draw the story of Paul's first missionary journey in a series of pictures as a strip cartoon. Pick out the most interesting events for your illustrations.

A biography to make

Make up from these references the story of Paul as a boy:

His home-town   Acts 9. 11; 21. 39; 22. 3

His parents and upbringing Acts 22. 25–28; 23. 6; 26. 5

Languages he spoke   Acts 21. 37; Acts 21. 40; 22. 2; 23. 6

His citizenship   Acts 22. 28

His trade   Acts 18. 3; 20. 34; 28. 30

His background of city life   1 Corinthians 3. 10; 10. 25; 9. 24–27; 14. 8; 2 Corinthians 10. 4; Romans 13. 6–7; Galatians 6. 17; Ephesians 6. 13–17.

To draw and describe

Paul describes an athlete, in 1 Corinthians 9. 24–25: and a soldier, in Ephesians 6. 11–18. Draw one of them, and describe why he was like a Christian.

To play a role

Imagine you were Mark and that you went with Barnabas, your uncle, and Paul on the missionary journey to Cyprus and to Asia Minor. Explain why you left them at Perga and went back home.

To find out

Paul appointed ministers for his churches. Find out the titles and work of some Christian ministers today. Describe what you find out.

To copy

Copy in ornamental script the passage in Paul's letter to the churches in Galatia, on the 'fruits of the Spirit' (Galatians 5. 22–23).

Jews and Gentiles in the Church

Paul's return to the Church at Antioch

It was the year C.E. 47 when Paul and Barnabas returned to Syrian Antioch from the first missionary journey. They were given a great welcome by the church. Everyone was thrilled by the story that they told. During their two years of travel they had covered 2250 km by land and sea. They had spread the Gospel in the island of Cyprus and on the mainland of Asia Minor. God had richly blessed their work. Jews had often opposed them and tried to hinder their work. But Gentiles had heard them gladly. God had given them faith and the power of his Spirit. Many, both Jews and Gentiles, had been baptised. Many new churches had been established. One thing the missionaries had learnt more than anything else—God welcomed Gentiles into his Church.

The Christians at Antioch were delighted by this. The majority of them were Gentiles. Their church had been founded by Hellenist Jews who had left Jerusalem when persecution had begun against them. They had a wider outlook than the Jews of Judaea and closer contacts with Gentiles. They had gladly preached the Christian message to Gentiles, and many had chosen to follow the faith in Jesus. In their church at Antioch, Jews and Gentiles met together. They worshipped together and ate together at the meal of fellowship.

It was very different in the church at Jerusalem. Its members

THE CHALICE OF ANTIOCH

The most famous discovery from Syrian Antioch is this chalice, or cup, used at the communion service. It was found in 1910 by Arabs digging a well. The outside silver case, decorated with 12 figures, encloses an inner cup, hammered out from a strip of silver, that would contain over two litres of liquid. The outer chalice rises 20 cm above the stem, and is made of carved silverwork. The chalice dates from about C.E. 400, but the cup it was made to contain must have been older and greatly valued. It is certainly the oldest known Christian chalice.

were mostly Hebrews, Jews of Judaea, once the Hellenists had left the city. They tended to be narrow in their outlook; they lived strictly by the sacred Law; they had nothing to do with Gentiles. They did believe, however, that their Jewish Messiah had come in Jesus. God had proved it by raising him from the dead. In him they saw all the hopes and prophecies of the Jews fulfilled. This was the message that they preached to their fellow Jews. They should accept their Messiah and enter into their heritage in his kingdom. All this had nothing to do with Gentiles. To them, Christians were Jews who accepted Jesus as their Messiah. The Christian Church was a sect of Jews.

Thus, it was quite unthinkable for the Christians at Jerusalem to admit Gentiles into the Church—unless, of course, they were proselytes who had accepted the Jewish Law and become full Jews. We have read of one strange happening, when Peter had been called to preach to a household of Romans at Caesarea. It was true that they had believed in Jesus and the power of his Spirit had come upon them. But that was an exception. It would be quite a different matter for Jews and Gentiles to mix together in the Church. But that was exactly what seemed to be happening in Antioch. Christians at Jerusalem were appalled when they heard about it. They had sent Barnabas to Antioch to find out what was happening there. He was a Hellenist from Cyprus, but he was a loyal Jew on whom they could rely. Barnabas was quite carried away by what he found at Antioch. The church there was full of life and eager to spread the Gospel. Barnabas gladly joined in it, mixing happily with Gentiles in worship and at table. Here was a great opportunity for missionary work. He needed someone to help him, and at once his thoughts turned to Paul of Tarsus. He went up to Tarsus and brought Paul back with him. For two years they worked together at Antioch, side by side, preaching the Gospel to Jews and Gentiles alike.

The Churches of Antioch and Jerusalem

Barnabas had to report back to the church at Jerusalem on the church at Antioch. The opportunity came in C.E. 46 when news reached Antioch of famine in Judaea. Naturally the members of the church wanted to help their fellow-Christians at Jerusalem. But it was not just a matter of giving them charity. Christians at Jerusalem had, from the very beginning, deliberately lived in poverty. They had sold all their possessions and given the money to the church. They believed that they should own nothing. They lived frugally, content with the bare necessities of life. In Antioch the Gentile Christians did not choose this way of life, but they honoured their fellow-Christians at Jerusalem for choosing the way of poverty. They showed their respect by helping to supply their needs. This was a matter of religious devotion, not simply of giving charity.

As we saw, Barnabas and Paul were chosen to take the collection to Jerusalem. There they met privately with Peter and James and John, the three leading apostles, to discuss their work. It was agreed that they should carry on as they had been. The three apostles would continue their preaching among Jews of Judaea. Paul and Barnabas would continue their work at Antioch among both Jews and Gentiles. Nothing was decided about Jews and Gentiles mixing together in one church. The three apostles could hardly claim to control churches founded among Gentiles by Paul and Barnabas. In any case, they had never had anything to do with Gentiles, except for Peter's strange experience at Caesarea.

One thing was agreed at this meeting. Christians at Antioch would go on helping the Christians in Jerusalem who lived in deliberate poverty. This would be a bond of unity between the two churches.

Peter   **Paul**

EARLY PORTRAITS OF THE APOSTLES

Peter at Antioch

Peter does not seem to have said anything definite at this meeting about Gentiles in the Church. He was the only apostle to have mixed with them. He knew that the Spirit of God had come to them. But he does not seem to have made up his mind about the place of Gentiles in the Church. In fact, he seems to have been just as impetuous and changeable as he had been during the ministry of Jesus. When he was in Jerusalem he lived as a Jew, working with the other apostles among Jews. But it was different when he went to Antioch.

Peter visited Antioch, later, when Paul and Barnabas had returned from their missionary journey. There he joined happily in the life of the church. He worshipped with Gentile Christians. He ate with them at table—a thing no strict Jew could possibly do, for it would be breaking the sacred Law of God. But during Peter's stay a party of Jewish Christians came from Jerusalem to Antioch. It does not seem that they had been sent officially by the other apostles. But they naturally had great influence and they were respected as members of the very first Christian church. They were strict Jews and they would not dream of breaking the Law by eating with Gentiles. They ate separately, having their own meal of fellowship. Peter joined them. So too did other Jewish Christians, including Barnabas. Now the church at Antioch was split. Jews and Christians were meeting separately.

Paul was appalled by this. He was very angry to see the church divided into Jews and Gentiles. He challenged Peter, face to face, in front of all the others. He saw clearly that the meal of fellowship and the remembrance of the Last Supper were the centre of the life of the church. If Jews and Gentiles could not meet there, bound together by their faith in Jesus, they met nowhere.

Peter tried to suggest a compromise. He proposed that Jews and Gentiles should continue to meet separately for the common meal. Paul rejected the idea at once. This would make Jews superior to Gentiles in the Church. Gentile Christians would be like God-fearers in the Jewish synagogue—not full members. They would not become full members until they accepted the Jewish Law. Paul openly criticised Peter. He had been happily mixing with Gentiles in the church at Antioch, breaking the Jewish Law. In that case

THE JEWISH LAW ON KOSHER AND UNKOSHER FOOD

Animals

Kosher

(a) Have a split hoof, and

(b) Chew the cud,

   e.g. ox, sheep, deer, giraffe etc.

Unkosher

(a) Chew the cud but do not have split hoof, e.g. hare.

(b) Have split hoof but do not chew the cud, e.g. pigs.

(c) Have no hooves, e.g. dogs, cats.

Birds, Reptiles and Insects

Kosher

Domestic fowl

Unkosher

(a) Most birds of prey

(b) All reptiles

(c) Insects (except some locusts)

Fish

Kosher

Those with fins, scales and backbones

Unkosher

Shellfish, crabs, shrimps, shark, etc.

See Deuteronomy 14.3–20;

Leviticus 11.2–23 and 41–47

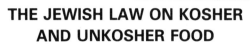

the Law could not be very important to him. Then why did he expect Gentiles to accept the Law?

There was another serious problem too. The Christian Jews from Jerusalem were saying that Gentile Christians must accept the Jewish Law and become full Jews. This meant that they must be circumcised. This was a small operation on the penis of every Jewish boy, made soon after birth (Genesis 17. 9–13; Leviticus 12. 3; Luke 2. 21). This was the mark of the Jew, the outward sign of being one of the people of God. Gentiles did not agree with this custom and probably disliked it because of their tradition of venerating the human body. That was why many Gentiles became God-fearers but few became full Jews. Certainly very few Gentiles would become Christians if they had first to accept the Jewish Law. They might also have objected to the Jewish food laws, which were alien to them; to the sabbath laws, to which they were not accustomed.

All these problems added up to one question—must Gentiles become Jews in order to enter the Christian Church? Paul decided that the matter must be thrashed out, once and for all. The church at Antioch agreed that a party should go to Jerusalem to settle the matter with the apostles and leaders of the church there. Paul and Barnabas were the natural leaders.

Paul's letter to the Galatians

The party from Antioch travelled to Jerusalem overland. They came down along the coast road, through Phoenicia and then through Samaria—a district that most Jews would avoid because of its danger to them. They were welcomed by all the churches

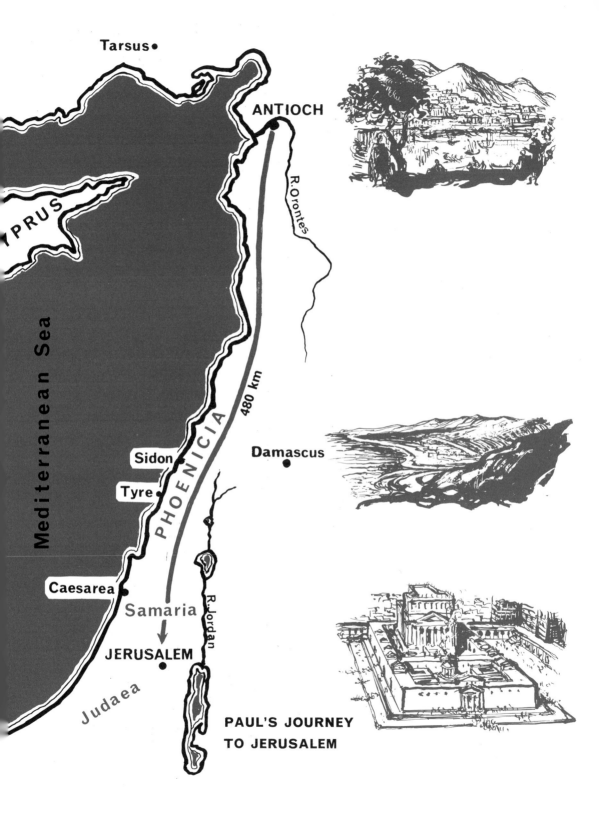

Tarsus•

ANTIOCH

R. Orontes

CYPRUS

Mediterranean Sea

PHOENICIA

480 km

Sidon

Tyre

Damascus•

Caesarea

R. Jordan

Samaria

JERUSALEM•

Judaea

**PAUL'S JOURNEY
TO JERUSALEM**

along their journey. We do not know who founded these churches in Phoenicia and Samaria, but they show how the Gospel was spreading abroad. Christians in these lands were filled with joy when they heard how Gentiles were being won to the Church. But there is no mention of any welcome for Paul and his party from the churches in Judaea.

It may have been on this journey that Paul wrote his hurried and angry Letter to the Galatians, included in the New Testament. It may have been written two or three years later. But what matters about this letter is that it is concerned with this problem of Jews and Gentiles in the Christian Church. It was sent to the churches which Paul and Barnabas had founded in Asia Minor on the first missionary journey—the churches at Antioch in Pisidia, Iconium, Lystra and Derbe. Jewish Christians, possibly from Jerusalem, had been visiting these churches. They had been contradicting Paul's teaching. They had questioned his authority. They had challenged his right to be a leader in the Church.

Paul had taught the pagan Gentiles of Asia Minor that the great moment in all history had come. In the beginning, God had promised to Abraham, the great father of the Jewish people, that all nations would be blessed through him. This was long before the Law had ever been heard of. Now God had kept his promise. He had acted. He had sent his Son into the world. The death of Jesus had changed everything between men and God. He had been raised from the dead; he reigns as Lord. All mankind belong to him. By believing in him, by entrusting their lives to him, men became sons of God. They entered into his family, the 'household of faith'. In God's family all lived together as one—Jews and Gentiles, slaves and freemen, rich and poor, educated and

A MANUSCRIPT OF PAUL'S LETTERS

This is the oldest manuscript known of the Letters of Paul. It comes from the Chester Beatty Papyri found in the south of Egypt. The papyri were laid flat, as in a book, instead of being wound in scrolls, making a 'codex'. They date from about C.E. 200.

uneducated, men and women. God gave his Spirit to all who believed. His Spirit changed their lives. They had a new ideal for living, and the power of the Spirit to help them live up to it.

The Jewish Christians were teaching something quite different. They said that believing in Jesus was only the first step for Gentiles. Being baptised and receiving the Spirit of God were not enough. Gentiles must accept the sacred Law of God if they wanted to share in his promises. They must be circumcised, they must keep Jewish food-laws, they must observe Jewish feasts, they must keep the strict laws of the sabbath. Paul had been quite wrong in ignoring these parts of true religion. He had said nothing about them because he wanted to make Christianity easier and more attractive to Gentiles. In any case, Paul was not a genuine apostle. His only authority came from the true apostles at Jerusalem. How could he be trusted when he went against their teachings?

These attacks on Paul and on his teaching had met with success. All his work was being undermined. His Letter to the Galatians was his reply. He wrote with passion and with anger, for he saw that his teaching about the Gospel was at stake. It was Jesus himself who had given him his authority. Jesus had called him to be an apostle on the road to Damascus. He was not dependent on the apostles at Jerusalem—indeed, he had already had to challenge Peter face to face, and to rebuke him. But the apostles had certainly approved of his work when he had met them at Jerusalem.

But something much more important was at stake than Paul's authority. The Gospel message of Christianity was that Jesus had died to bring men to God. They were saved by faith in Jesus—not by keeping the Law. The Galatians themselves had received the

Spirit of God when they believed. The Law of the Jews acted like a guardian. It had brought up the Jews, teaching them their way of life. Christians learned their way of life through the Spirit of Jesus and were full members of the household of God. They were free to live as his sons, doing their Father's will, therefore Christian Jews did not need the guardianship of the Law any more.

This was Paul's argument. He felt that the Law was no longer necessary. Men entered the church of God by baptism—not by circumcision. His Church was not just a sect of the Jews. If it was, then Christianity was no different from Judaism. Jesus said he had come to save all men and that his Church was for all mankind.

The Council of Jerusalem, C.E. 49

It was in the year C.E. 49 that Paul and his party came to Jerusalem to settle this great problem of Jews and Gentiles in the Christian Church. Paul and Barnabas gave a full account of their work to the assembly of Christians at Jerusalem. But, hardly had they finished, when strict Jews challenged them. They insisted that Gentiles must become full Jews and accept the Jewish Law if they wished to enter the Church. A further meeting was arranged for the leaders to decide on the problem.

The 'chairman' at this official meeting was James. This was not

James the apostle—he had already died a martyr's death (Acts 12. 1–2). This was the eldest of the four brothers of Jesus (Mark 6. 3). All the brothers had opposed Jesus during his ministry (Mark 3. 31–35). But James at least was now a member of the Church. It was natural to give special respect to a brother of the Lord, and James was now the 'head' of the church at Jerusalem. He was a devout Jew, known as 'James the Just', and later tradition said that he died a martyr for his faith.

The meeting of the leaders began with discussion. Then Peter related his experience at Caesarea, when the Spirit of God came upon Cornelius, the Roman officer, and his household. If therefore God made no difference between Jew and Gentile, in giving his Spirit, how could they? Paul and Barnabas believing and receiving the Spirit of God. Then James spoke. He did not simply sum up the discussion, as the chairman of a meeting would today. He spoke with authority. It was his decision, not the result of everyone voting. God would speak through him. The spirit of the meeting would be expressed in his words.

James stated, first, that Gentiles were not to be troubled. They did not need to be circumcised or to accept the Jewish Law. Thus, Jews and Gentiles were not to be separated in any way in the life of the Church. They would mix together, worship together and share the meal of fellowship together.

But the conscience of Jewish Christians must be safeguarded. There must be no trace of pagan ways in the Church. Gentiles, once they became Christians, must have nothing more to do with their former pagan customs. Pagans offered animals as sacrifices to their gods. Part of the meat would be used in the temple of the god. The rest would be eaten at a banquet, following the sacrifice,

PAGANS SACRIFICING TO THEIR GODS

This carving on a Roman tomb shows a cock being sacrificed to the god Dionysius, or Bacchus, the Greek and Roman god of wine and of fertility.

and sold in the market. Gentile Christians must not join in these banquets. They must not buy any meat that had been offered to pagan gods. Thus, Christian Jews would not have to fear breaking the Law when they ate with Gentile Christians in each other's houses and in the fellowship meal.

Finally, James ordered that Gentile Christians were to have nothing more to do with the immoral ways of pagans. Jews were not only disgusted by pagan worship. They were also horrified by the moral evils which accompanied pagan worship. Shameful sexual practices were not just the result of over-eating and over-drinking at pagan feasts. They were part of the worship itself. Gentile Christians must live pure lives, giving up all their former ways. Then they would give no offence to Jews, brought up in the strict morality of the Law, when they mixed together in the Christian Church.

Official letters were written stating these decisions. They were addressed to the Gentile Churches of Asia Minor. They were to be taken to Antioch in Syria by two leading members of the Jerusalem church. One was Judas Barsabas, a Jew of Judaea. The other was Silas, a Hellenist Jew from abroad and a Roman citizen. This was a good choice, for they represented both groups of Jews. The letters gave them their authority. They would be able to give the decisions of the Council by word of mouth––the spoken word was much more highly regarded, in those times, than the written word. They would also be able to explain any details about the decisions. The visit to Antioch of these two important members of the Jerusalem church did something more. It showed the brotherhood between the two churches. Silas was, in fact, to remain at Antioch and to accompany Paul on his second missionary journey.

THE TAKING OF JERUSALEM

The Emperor Vespasian

The results of the Council

This was the very first Council of the Christian Church. It included representatives of all the churches which existed. Thus it is called an ECUMENICAL Council. This comes from the Greek word 'oiku-mene' which meant 'the inhabited world'. Thus, ECUMENICAL means WORLD-WIDE. It is a very common and important word today, when the various Christian Churches work together in the modern ECUMENICAL MOVEMENT.

It was through the work of Paul that the Christian Church became worldwide. The Council of Jerusalem had been a great victory for his beliefs. Jews and Gentiles could now live happily together in the Christian Church. Luke, in The Acts of the Apostles, implies that the Council settled everything and brought peace to the Church. But we know from Paul's letters that this did not happen. There followed a long and bitter struggle. Paul was persecuted all through his life for what he believed.

The struggle went on until C.E. 70 when the long war between Jews and Romans ended with the destruction of Jerusalem. Christian Jews fled to Pella, a Greek city of the Decapolis, east of the river Jordan. A further Jewish revolt ended in C.E. 135 with the banishment of the Jews from their homeland. But by that time the Christian Church had spread throughout the Roman world and among Gentiles of all races.

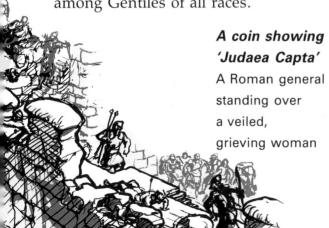

A coin showing 'Judaea Capta'
A Roman general standing over a veiled, grieving woman

Paul was to go on from the Council to at least two further great missionary journeys which brought Christianity to Europe, and to Rome itself. His travels are vividly described by Luke, now his companion, in eyewitness accounts. But we hear no more of Peter. Later Christian historians record that both he and Paul died at

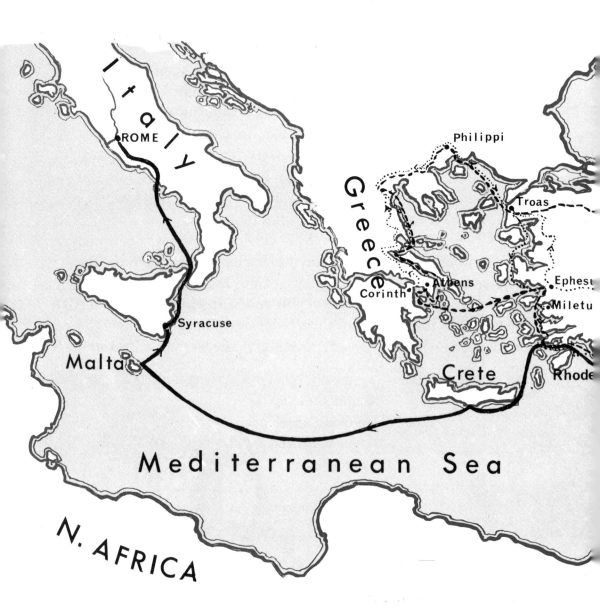

Rome in the persecution under the emperor Nero in C.E. 64. Tradition said that Peter was crucified and buried in the cemetery near Nero's Circus. The great Christian church of St. Peter's was built there, and in modern times the tomb of Peter has been found beneath it.

PAUL THE MISSIONARY

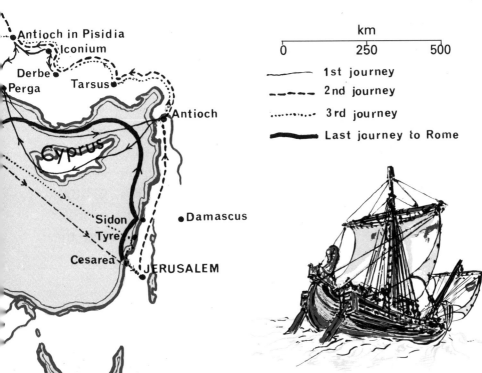

Antioch in Pisidia
Iconium
Derbe
Perga
Tarsus
Antioch
Cyprus
Sidon
Tyre
Damascus
Cesarea
JERUSALEM

km

0   250   500

—————— 1st journey

— — — — 2nd journey

············· 3rd journey

━━━━━ Last journey to Rome

THE TOMB OF PETER

Excavations, below the crypt of St. Peter's in Rome, brought to light this memorial built over the grave of Peter about C.E. 160.

Luke's book, The Acts of the Apostles, recounted the story of how the Church spread from Jerusalem to Rome, the capital of the whole empire. The main hero of his story is Paul, the 'Apostle of the Gentiles'. He had lived and died for the Church, fighting to extend the interpretation of Christianity. Through his work it became a universal Church, welcoming men of all nations into the family of God.

To find and read in your Bible

The church at Antioch	Acts 11. 19–26.
The churches of Antioch and Jerusalem	Acts 11. 29–30; Galat-ians 2. 1–2 and 9–10.
Peter at Antioch	Galatians 2. 11–14.
Jewish Christians at Antioch	Acts 15. 1–2.
Paul leads a party to Jerusalem	Acts 15. 3–4.
The Council of Jerusalem	Acts 15. 6–12.
James makes decisions	Acts 15. 13–21.
Letters and delegates go to Antioch	Acts 15. 22–35.

To discuss

Discuss the way in which Christians at Jerusalem lived deliberately in poverty, like monks, owning nothing. What good can you see in living like that? What can we learn from it?

To compare

Compare the characters of Peter and Paul. What did they have in common? What differences were there between them? If you can, draw a portrait of each of them to show what kind of man you think each of them was.

To design

Design a chart, with your own drawings, of the kosher and unkosher foods of the Jewish Law.

A letter to write

Imagine you were Paul, keeping in touch with his churches in Galatia. Write the letter which you would have sent.

To act

Act the scene when Peter was at Antioch and Paul accused him for his change of attitude towards Gentiles. The main characters will be Peter and Paul. The followers of each of them can add to the discussion, too.

To report

Imagine that you were a reporter at Jerusalem, covering the Council of Jerusalem for your readers. Explain what the Council had met to decide, describe the main characters taking part in it, and give an account of the decisions that were reached.

To play a role

Imagine that you were a Gentile who had become a Christian. Describe what your previous religion was like, and how Christianity differs from it. Explain why you were attracted to Christianity.

To map

Make your own map of one of the journeys of Paul. You will be able to read about his second and third journeys in the next book in this series, *The Church of Jesus Grows*.

To research

Find out all you can about the Ecumenical Movement in the Christian Churches today. Why do you think the Churches are working together in this way?

To write out and remember

Write out, in illuminated script if you like, one or more of these fine passages from Paul's Letters. Writing them out will help you to remember them.

Baptism in Christ	Galatians 3. 26–28
Risen with Christ	Colossians 3. 1–2 and 12–14
A greeting	Galatians 1. 3–5
Sons of God	Romans 8. 14–17
Glory to God	Ephesians 3. 20–21.

To model

Make an imitation scroll, and write on it the decisions made at the Council of Jerusalem. You can copy them from the Bible or express them in your own words.

To play a role

Imagine that you were a Gentile member of the Church at Antioch when Paul came back from the Council with Silas and Judas Barsabas. Why was everyone so full of joy?

To explain

Explain the meaning of these words which you have read in this chapter. Some of them you have already had before, so this will be a test of your reading: chalice; Hellenists; Hebrews; Dionysius; food laws; codex; Decapolis; Ecumenical Movement.

Index

159